FOREIGN RELATIONS

Memories of Germany and England

Alexander Oldham (né Oppenheim) was born into a wealthy Jewish family in Berlin in 1925. To escape Nazi persecution, he emigrated in 1937 to England, where he completed his education. At 17, he joined the British Army and served in the allied advance into Belgium and the Netherlands, and after the war in the British Mandate of Palestine. In 1947, he took British nationality, and lived for the rest of his life in the London area, where he was a successful businessman and, with his wife Jill, raised three children. He died in London in 2010.

FOREIGN RELATIONS

Memories of Germany and England

ALEXANDER OLDHAM

Marble Hill London

First published by Marble Hill Publishers in 2024

Flat 58 Macready House
75 Crawford Street
London W1H 5LP
www.marblehillpublishers.co.uk

Originally published privately in 2015.

Text © The Estate of Alexander Oldham 2024

The moral rights of the copyright owners have been asserted, in accordance with the Copyright, Designs and Patents Act 1988.

All rights reserved.

No part of this book may be reproduced or transmitted in any form or by any means, electronic, mechanical, recording or otherwise, without prior written permission of the copyright owners.

A CIP catalogue record for this book is available from the British Library.

ISBN: 9781739265786

Text and cover design by Paul Harpin
Printed and bound by IngramSpark

TABLE OF CONTENTS

Foreword	vi
Dedication	vii
GERMANY	1
Introduction	3
1. Berlin 1925	5
2. The Golden Years	23
3. Change	43
4. Darkening Skies	79
ENGLAND AND THE WAR	91
5. Emigration	92
6. Settling In	100
7. The British Army	109
8. Towards an Uncertain Future	137
MARIA'S STORY	138
Escape from Berlin	139

FOREWORD

Our father Alexander (or Alec, as he was known) wrote the first part of this memoir of his early life in 1992. His aim was to capture the facts and the flavour of his privileged life in Berlin, of which he had sharp and vivid memories, as a legacy for us. He bashed it out on a manual typewriter and pasted in photocopies of images from his extraordinary collection of family photographs. He later added the final section to the manuscript, concerning his service in the army.

When Dad died in London in 2010 at the age of eighty-five, we shared his memoirs (still in the hand- and type-written form in which he wrote them) with a few people who had known him. One such person was Frances's friend Naomi Clifford, who immediately said that Dad's story, unusual in that it is a vivid depiction of a former life that few others survived, let alone recorded, was worthy of publication. She single-handedly converted it into a wonderfully produced book, adding some interesting editorial notes. We are truly indebted to Naomi for her generosity, skill and dedication, without which this "bridge to our Continental past" would still be in a ring-binder, known only to us. The fact that it will reach a wider audience in this new, published form would have delighted Dad, as it does us.

Frances, Jacqueline and Peter
London, January 2024

The footnotes are Alexander's except where indicated.

DEDICATION

I DEDICATE THIS memoir of my childhood in Berlin between 1925, the year of my birth, and 1937, the year of my emigration, to my children, Frances, Jacqueline and Peter.

In the line of our family's descent from Daniel Itzig (1733-1799), the Jewish money broker who rose to become Chancellor of the Prussian Royal Mint, they are the first generation in two hundred and fifty years to be born British.

When circumstances occur in history that force entire communities to flee their native country, change their names and adopt new nationalities, all in the span of one decade, family accounts are frequently lost to future generations. These reminiscences are intended to act as a bridge to our Continental past.

Alexander Oldham né Oppenheim
London, December 1992

FOREIGN RELATIONS

GERMANY

FOREIGN RELATIONS

INTRODUCTION

THE YEAR 1925 saw the beginning of a revival in Germany, after the ravages of the post world war hyperinflation, which at its climax in 1923 had seen the value of the mark against the dollar decline from its pre-war level of 4.2 marks to one dollar to 4,200,000,000,000 marks. As early as 1920, the victorious Allies were forced to reduce the war reparations of the Versailles Treaty from 209 billion gold marks to 132 billion, to be paid over a period of thirty-five years. But with Germany totally incapable of meeting these demands, the French occupied the Rhineland and annexed the strategic coal and steel industries of the Ruhr. This led to the greatest inflation the world had ever seen, with the German government resorting to the printing presses in an ever-increasing debasement of the currency, thereby achieving simultaneously the ruination of the German middle class and the cessation of any meaningful reparation payments to the Allies.

The US government had increasingly distanced itself from the revanchist French position, being fearful of the possibility of Germany succumbing to a second post-war Communist coup. The US Senate passed an amendment to the 1920 Dawes plan,[1] and the German government collaborated by linking the value of the mark to the value of land. The new currency, the Rentenmark, was underpinned by massive American loans and was fixed at one new mark to one trillion paper marks.

This historic devaluation was the work of Dr Hjalmar Schacht who was appointed special commissioner to restore the

---

1 When Germany defaulted on its First World War reparations payments, American banker Charles G. Dawes was asked by the Allies to investigate. In 1924 he proposed a plan for instituting annual payments of reparations on a fixed scale. He also recommended the reorganisation of the German State Bank and increased foreign loans. *(Ed.)*

currency three days after Hitler's unsuccessful Munich putsch of 12 November 1923. The success of the restoration of the currency led to the evacuation of the Ruhr, the Locarno Pact guaranteeing Germany's western borders with France and Belgium, Germany's admission to the League of Nations, and the evacuation of the first zone of the demilitarised Rhineland by French troops.

Dr Schacht was later to become a member of the Nazi Party and be appointed Finance Minister in Hitler's first administration. Germany's inflation was brought to an abrupt halt, but at a huge political and human price, which planted the seeds of World War Two.

In Britain, Churchill, as Chancellor of the Exchequer, had returned sterling to the gold standard in 1925, a measure that was to make Britain highly uncompetitive and contributed to massive outflows of gold from the reserves to the US. It also created a spiral of competitive pressures on British labour costs, leading to the industrial unrest which culminated in the general strike of 1926.

Britain's self-imposed problems accrued to Germany's advantage. Although the old currency had been abolished overnight, and the savings of millions wiped out, the industrialists and bankers of the Weimar Republic now had a firm base on which to rebuild their own, and their country's, fortunes, helped by huge American investment flowing into the country. 1925 ushered in the few golden years of the unstable post-war German political era, until the Wall Street crash of 1929 plunged first America and then every Western economy into the Great Depression. In Germany's case, this enabled Hitler to take power in 1933 on a tide of resentment against the November 1918 capitulation, which he singled out as the primary cause of Germany's betrayal by its politicians, and the consequent sufferings of the German people under the yoke of the Versailles Treaty.

CHAPTER ONE
BERLIN

1925 WAS THE year I was born in Berlin, and in many ways the circumstances of my family reflected the mores of the times. Berlin's population of about four million included some three hundred thousand German Jews, a figure at least twenty-five per cent lower than that which would have been reached by the inclusion of the baptised German Jews, precisely as, to their horror and disbelief, the Nazis were to count their numbers under the decrees of the Nuremberg race laws.

Pre-1933 Germany was unique in Europe in not only assimilating its Jewish population, in the cause of the national interest, a philosophy shared to a less obvious extent by England, but also in encouraging prominent Jewish families to convert to the Lutheran evangelism that constituted, at least in Prussia and its capital Berlin, the unofficial state religion. In the Rhineland and Bavaria, where the majority of the population adhered to the Catholic faith, there was a far lower rate of Jewish conversion, and a markedly greater degree of antisemitism.

The relatively liberal internal policies adopted by Bismarck under Kaiser Wilhelm I, and later continued by Wilhelm II, were primarily directed at the creation of a German national identity and patriotism to which the loyalties and aspirations of all its citizens were harnessed. Whilst the political levers of power were largely in the hands of the aristocratic Junker[1] families, the valuable potential of the German Jewish intelligentsia and business community was both recognised and encouraged to play its part in the German expansionary policies of the pre-1914 era. Unlike France, where antisemitic feeling led to discrimination

1 Members of the landed nobility in Prussia.

against Jews at every level of society, Germany permitted its Jewish citizens to rise to positions of influence and power. Moreover, and increasingly after 1870, Jews who converted to the Lutheran religion immeasurably improved their standing in the corridors of power in the new imperial Germany.

This explains to some extent the apparent anomaly between some classes of Jews who converted and others who did not. Jewish doctors and artists, as well as scientists and writers, continued on the whole to conform to the Judaic tradition, as demand for their services was measured by their abilities in direct ratio with their reputation and success. Lacking these individual attributes, Jewish civil servants, professional soldiers, industrialists and bankers were clearly able to benefit from the increased patronage of the German ruling classes by belonging to the right club, and the higher conversion rate among such groups reflected this situation.

MY FATHER, ROBERT Hugo Oppenheim, was the youngest of five children, and the only boy, born into a wealthy Berlin banking family. His mother Anna was also born an Oppenheim[2] and was a first cousin of her husband Hugo Oppenheim. Both my paternal grandparents inherited a Christian conversion from at least two generations of baptised Jews. My great-grandfather, Otto Georg Oppenheim,[3] had married Margarethe Mendelssohn, a direct descendant from that equally converted family of bankers who

---

[2] Grandfather Hugo's parents were Georg Oppenheim, a tribunal judge from Königsberg, who married Margarethe Mendelssohn of Berlin; and Grandmother Anna's parents were Rudolph Alexander Oppenheim (after whom I was named), also from Königsberg, who married Dorothea von Heimann, who was born in 1828, in Vilnius, Lithuania, then part of Russia. Alexander was a disciple of Ferdinand Lasalle, the [Jewish] protagonist of the workers' movement and defender of the poor. To help Lasalle, Alexander, assisted by a relation from the Mendelssohn family, stole some documents from a Count Ratzfeldt, intending to compromise the count. This became a highly publicised scandal and, despite Lasalle's vigorous defence of his two followers, Alexander was sent to prison. He was soon released when Alexander van Humboldt, a friend of the Mendelssohns, intervened with the King.

[3] For Otto Georg Oppenheim's life in the Villa Oppenheim in Berlin–Charlottenburg see Felix Gilbert's *A European Past: Memoirs 1905–1945* (Norton & Co., New York, 1988). [Felix Gilbert was a member of the Mendelssohn-Bartholdy family. – *Ed.*]

traced their line indirectly to the composer Felix Mendelssohn-Bartholdy, himself a baptised Jew.[4]

The Mendelssohns and Oppenheims intermarried in various branches of their descendants, each adopting the Lutheran religion. It is a particular irony that their frantic attempts to rid themselves of their Jewish origins over a period of a hundred and fifty years did not prevent Hitler from banning all performances of that 'Jewish' composer's music from the German repertoire after 1933.

My grandparents, first cousins Hugo and Anna Oppenheim, each had brothers and sisters. One of these was Franz Oppenheim, well known at the time as the founder of the AGFA chemical and photographic combine. Grandfather Hugo, who died in 1921 at the age of 74, exactly the same age at which my father died in 1956, was the founder of the family bank, Hugo Oppenheim & Sohn. In German this was called a Handelsbank, in structure and scope closer to a French banque d'affaires than the larger and more prestigious British merchant banks with the old established names of Barings, Hambros or Lazards.

With the financial backing from Franz's industrial enterprises, Hugo developed a close link for the bank with the Tsarist government, which was looking to Europe to provide capital for the infrastructure to bring Russia into the industrialised world of the late nineteenth century. The Russian railway construction programme, in particular, was a regular borrower in the sterling, French franc and German mark bond markets and Hugo Oppenheim & Sohn took up and underwrote many such issues – so much so that Grandfather Hugo would receive, from time to time, token gifts from the Tsar's personal office as a mark of appreciation. These took the form of Fabergé trinkets, or diamond jewellery for my grandmother, and were always accompanied by a personal message from the court chamberlain. Sadly, none of

---

4   Felix Gilbert's book *Bankiers, Künstler und Gelehrte* [Mohr Siebeck, 1975]
(unpublished letters from the Mendelssohn family in the 19th century) includes a photograph of Felix Mendelssohn's grave on which is mounted a cross, leaving no doubt that he was raised in the Lutheran faith.

these gifts remain in the family, either here or in America.

Grandfather Hugo, having followed his father into the lifestyle of a baptised Jew, had long forgotten, if indeed he ever knew, any of the formal tenets of the Jewish religion. His membership of the Lutheran community did not involve him in anything more arduous than a handsome annual contribution to the funds of the local evangelical church and the ritualistic trappings of a German Christmas, decorated tree and all.

Robert Hugo Oppenheim, my father, was born in Berlin in 1882 and, after a conventional private school education, was despatched in 1901, aged 19, to Balliol College, Oxford. This was then not all that unusual, as the great British universities were not yet subsidised by the state and, needing to provide adequate numbers of scholarships to British grammar school entrants, accepted a sizeable enrolment of foreign students who paid the full fees. Knowing that these young men came mainly, although not exclusively, for the pleasures of Oxbridge life, often not staying for the full course of the degree, the university did not erect particularly high academic barriers to their entry.

My father's time at Oxford was marked by a determined attempt on his part to outshine the British upper classes in all but intellectual pursuits. He was accompanied by a valet and several steamer trunks containing formal apparel, riding gear and polo equipment. He hired two polo ponies from a local livery stable and settled down to a life of conspicuous ostentation, without, as far as is known, bothering to attend any lectures. Eventually, even Oxford's relaxed Edwardian attitude to the extravagances of its jeunesse dorée found this foreign exhibitionist too difficult to assimilate and, after eighteen months, the Master of Balliol wrote to my grandfather politely suggesting that his son might have a more promising career within a more dirigiste environment, such as a good regiment, German naturally.

Thus it turned out. On his return to Berlin, Father obtained a commission in one of the more prestigious cavalry regiments of Kaiser Wilhelm's army, the 15th Regiment of the Schleswig–Holstein Ulanen. Grandfather Hugo had himself served in the same regiment as a reserve officer in the Franco–Prussian war of 1870 to 1871 and had been decorated with the Iron Cross Second Class for his part in patrols in the front line. Father's expert horsemanship, coupled with access to Grandfather Hugo's generous financial subventions, guaranteed him popularity and success in the regiment. This could be likened to one of the British cavalry regiments of the line, not quite as elitist as the Blues and Royals, but certainly on a par with the Lancer, Dragoon and Hussar formations of the British Army of the day.

Father's regimental life, after the first year, was not a permanent occupation but continued in the style of the British Territorials, with recall to the colours for weekends and summer manoeuvres. Towards the end of the first decade of the twentieth century, therefore, he was gradually introduced to the work of the family bank, his apprenticeship made more agreeable by visits to the firm's foreign correspondents in Saint Petersburg, London, Paris and New York.

This pleasant and stimulating life continued right up to the eve of the First World War, just prior to which, in 1913, Father became engaged to Lotte (Charlotte) Simon, the daughter of one of Berlin's most influential intellectual Jewish families. His fiancée's father was an industrialist and amateur archaeologist who had financed some of the German expeditions to Egypt before the First World War and whose bust still stands in a place of honour in the entrance of Berlin's Egyptian museum (Ägyptisches Museum und Papyrussammlung) in Charlottenburg.[5]

Shortly after Father's marriage to Lotte Simon, war broke out. As a reservist officer, he rejoined his regiment with the higher rank of Rittmeister, equivalent to that of Major. He served throughout 1914 and 1915, on both the Russian and Western sectors, and took part in several front line engagements. For his conduct in action he was awarded the Iron Cross Second Class,

---

5 James Simon, a prominent patron of the arts, was the founder of the German Orient Gesellschafft (Orient Society). The Kaiser sought his advice on Near Eastern policy and on the administration of the new state museums. See *The Pity of It All: A Portrait of Jews in Germany 1743-1933* by Amos Elon (Allen Lane, 2002). (*Ed.*)

an honorable recognition at the time, and one which was to have a profound influence on my own life as a schoolboy in Hitler's Germany some twenty years later. By 1916 Father was nearly thirty-five years old and the combination of front line duty and his generally rather delicate health led to his honorable discharge on medical grounds, just before the first battle of the Somme.[6]

Father resumed his life with Lotte and in 1917 they had a son, whom they named Hugo after his grandfather. It could not have been foreseen that this boy would spend most of his formative childhood years not with his own mother but with his father's second wife, my own mother.

The marriage to Lotte was not particularly warm and her interests veered increasingly towards the artistic and intellectual community for which post-war Berlin was to provide such fertile ground. Lotte was not greatly involved with either her husband or her young son, and the marriage ended in divorce after Lotte left my father, not to return.

After the customary custody hearing, Father was adjudged the aggrieved party. He was by that time engaged to my mother and was, exceptionally for the time, awarded custody of Hugo, with the judge's proviso that my mother should agree to bring up Hugo as one of her own children. She undertook this, not just in the strict terms of the agreement but with unstinting love and affection for her stepson. This special relationship endured for all of Mother's long life and was reciprocated by Hugo in full measure. He regarded my mother as the only person who had ever given him genuine affection and stability during his adolescence and it was a tragedy for both, but especially for Hugo, that Father's waywardness ended this relationship in an abrupt separation eight years later, leaving Hugo, at the age of fifteen, with a trauma of desertion from which he never fully recovered.[7]

MY MOTHER, MARIA Helene Pinner, was the younger of two daughters born to a leading Jewish surgeon practising in

---

6 The first battle of the Somme started on 1 July 1916. *(Ed.)*

7 Hugo's mother, Lotte Simon, died in Germany in 1969. *(Ed.)*

Frankfurt, Geheimrat Dr Oskar Pinner, and his wife Anna, née Roos. Theirs was a typical fin de siècle bourgeois household at Bockenheimerlandstrasse 72, a large and slightly overfurnished town house in one of the most desirable parts of Frankfurt. The property was totally destroyed by bombs in 1943, and the ground on which it stood is now occupied by Chase Manhattan's offices.[8]

Mother's father was musically gifted and he used to play the violin in a small chamber group made up of friends and colleagues, whilst my grandmother ran the household, took appointments for his patients and supervised the excellent food. This was a mixture of Frankfurt specialities, such as Zwetschgenkuchen, a delicious damson flan unknown outside the region, and good old-fashioned Jewish noodle soup and dumplings. The Pinners employed a cook and a maid (the latter living in) but otherwise lived unostentatiously. Although Jewish, and brought up in the religious tradition of the synagogue, they had let their observance lapse without replacing it with anything else.

By 1925, when I was born, my Grandfather Pinner had only two more years to live, and I hardly remember him. Although comfortable and reasonably affluent, the Pinners had no car and not even a radio receiver, believing both to be unnecessary luxuries.[9] There is an anecdote that sums up my grandfather's lack of pretension. In German a top hat is called a Zylinder and is in fact a rigid type of opera hat. As in England at that time, black top hats were worn to formal occasions and as mourning attire. In the German language, however, the word Zylinder also describes the cylinders of internal combustion engines. In the racy parlance of the increasing number of motorists, cars were often referred to simply by the number of cylinders of their engines, so that the smallest might be two or four whilst the grandest boasted twelve or even sixteen cylinders. One day a wealthy patient arrived at

---

8 In 1992, when this memoir was written. *(Ed.)*

9 The only possessor of a primitive radio set was the house caretaker, Herr Salg. Once, when my aunt Erna was asked to give a talk about her South American travels on the recently opened Frankfurt radio transmitter, my grandmother asked Herr Salg to listen in. When she asked him later whether Erna's talk was good, he replied: 'Well, Frau Geheimrat, to be honest, it was not very interesting, but it was really loud!'

the surgery in his new car and proudly informed my grandfather that he now had an 'eight Zylinder.' As this failed to elicit any reaction, the patient persisted: 'Tell me, Herr Geheimrat, how many Zylinders do you have?' My grandfather was said to have replied with indifference, 'I have only one Zylinder, which I use for going to funerals. I hope I will not need to get it out for yours just yet.'

My mother, Maria Helene Pinner, was born in Frankfurt in 1891, eighteen months after her elder sister, Erna Wilhelmine, whose second name was chosen in honour of Kaiser Wilhelm II, another indication of the German Jewish intelligentsia's identification with the Fatherland and its monarchy.

The girls were educated in the local high school where, at quite an early age, Erna displayed a prodigious talent for drawing. Her school encouraged this to the point where the headmistress recommended that Erna should be sent to Paris to continue her studies under the best available teachers. This was a bold suggestion in a German provincial city such as Frankfurt in the first decade of the twentieth century, and it speaks volumes for my grandfather's liberal attitude that he agreed to send Erna to one of the leading art studios in Paris, the Académie Ranson. She was to remain there for three years, studying under Vuillard, Denis and Corinth, and only returned to Frankfurt just before war broke out in 1914.[10]

My mother, meanwhile, remained at home and, being both good-looking and possessed of an outgoing personality, soon entered into the young world of pre-war middle-class Frankfurt society. She also discovered a talent for sport and by the age of nineteen had won the ladies' amateur tennis championship held at the fashionable spa resort of Bad Ems. The prize was a handsome silver-plated Thermos jug, one of the earliest of its kind, engraved

---

10 The Académie Ranson was founded in Paris by the French painter Paul Ranson (1862–1909). Maurice Denis and Paul Sérusier delivered courses and Ker-Xavier Roussel, Félix Vallotton and Jean-Édouard Vuillard also attended, which added to its good reputation. After an unstable history through World War Two and beyond, it reopened in 1951 with new teachers. It finally closed in 1955 due to lack of funds. *(Ed.)*

with Mother's name, the venue and the year 1911. It remains in my possession and still functions perfectly.

At one of these forays into fashionable society meeting places, to which Mother was always accompanied by family friends, often in the company of other girls of her own age, she was introduced to Ernst Friedmann, a gentleman from Berlin who was taking a health cure. He was about fifteen years older than she and the co-proprietor of Friedmann & Weber, the leading interior design studio and workshop in Berlin. The company's reputation for flair and craftsmanship extended beyond Berlin to other major cities in Germany.

Whether Mother was swept off her feet or just impatient to leave the constricting atmosphere of family life in bourgeois Frankfurt for the glamour of life in Berlin I cannot say. She never discussed her life with Ernst Friedmann with me nor, to my knowledge, with any other member of our family. It seems at least possible that the reports of Erna's bohemian environment in Paris filtering back to Frankfurt may have inspired her. At any rate, Friedmann asked my grandparents for permission to marry their younger daughter. He evidently satisfied them as to his probity as well as to his ability to guarantee a lifestyle for his wife at least as comfortable as that enjoyed by the Pinner household – in the event it was far more so.

The fact that my mother never openly referred to this marriage until I was grown up, although she knew that I was aware of it from my aunt Erna, leads me to think that it was not particularly happy. I do not even know exactly when they were married but it must have been just before the First World War. They divorced about seven years later in what appears to have been an amicable parting on both sides.

In later life, when both Mother and Friedmann were living in London as refugees, Mother worked for him as an assistant. He was by then an old man eking out a living as an interior decorator among the Jewish émigrés of St John's Wood. Later she left him to set up in the same line of work on her own and they occasionally collaborated as business associates on a friendly basis. It was at that time that I first met Friedmann and I always remember that he was very solicitous about my progress at school and, later, in the Army. I could not have guessed that his interest was based on a far deeper relationship with my mother than that of a family friend 'from the old days' in Berlin, the public explanation Mother chose to use.

Exactly how and when my father and mother first met is not recorded. It must have been some time around 1920, when Father's marriage to Lotte Simon was breaking up and Mother was already divorced from Ernst Friedmann. Berlin was picking up the pieces after the austerities of four years of war, followed by a further year of street violence between left-wing anarchist and communist insurgents on one side, some led by disaffected naval units, and the notorious, extreme, right-wing Freikorps, a paramilitary organisation of former Army officers, on the other. Whilst the regular Army, the Reichswehr, reduced by the Versailles Treaty to a hundred thousand men, took no active part in these skirmishes, it lent moral support to the Freikorps, as did the civil police force. Only when the excesses of the Freikorps threatened to endanger the fragile constitution of the infant Weimar Republic, in the right-wing Kapp Putsch of 1920, did Friedrich Ebert, the Socialist first Chancellor of the Republic, command the Army to restore order. The years from 1920 to 1922 were therefore marked by a brief return to some sort of normality before the great inflation engulfed Germany in renewed chaos.

My parents were married in Berlin in 1921 and under the judicial separation agreement between Father and his first wife, Lotte Simon, their son Hugo, then five years old, came to live with my parents and was effectively brought up by my mother as her only child until my own arrival in January 1925.

The family home was a spacious apartment in a quiet residential area of West Berlin, flanked on one side by the beautiful Tiergarten and on the other by the Landwehrkanal, one of the picturesque waterways that wind their way through the heart of Berlin, between loops of the river Spree. We occupied the first floor of a large late nineteenth-century house which had been divided into three separate twelve-room apartments, one on each floor. The house was in the Matthäi-Kirchstrasse, a crescent whose curved arm enveloped a large and uniquely ugly brick church, the Lutheran Evangelical St Matthäi-Kirche, where I was baptised three weeks after my birth.[11]

The congregation reflected the relaxed attitude of the German Establishment towards its Jewish converts. Although I was too young to appreciate the nuances of the arrangements, I gathered later from my half brother Hugo that the framework within which baptised Jews mingled with the Christian descendants of the Lutheran tradition was one of tolerant uninterest in each other, in the manner of a members' club with liberal admission rules, rather than a community of militant Protestant Christianity.

My paternal grandfather Hugo had, in the 1880s, with great foresight, purchased a large plot of land next to the Brandenburger Tor which stood at the head of the Unter den Linden, the famous avenue of limes planted by Kaiser Wilhelm I. This symbolic thoroughfare became the equal of any of the great city avenues of Europe. The Brandenburger Tor was the focal point of all the great military parades and state visits in Imperial Germany before 1914. Processions passing through the arches of the Brandenburger Tor from the direction of the statue-lined Siegesallee (Victory Mall), which Wilhelm I had built to commemorate Prussia's defeat of France in 1871, would first enter a large three-sided square, which led at its open end into the Unter den Linden before reaching the Imperial Palace some two kilometres further east.

This square was the Pariser Platz and without doubt it was the most desirable location in Berlin after the Imperial Palace itself and the chancelleries of the Wilhelmstrasse. It was reserved for the Imperial civil service. Hugo Oppenheim first lived in

11 The whole area of the Matthäi-Kirchstrasse was totally destroyed by Allied bombing in World War Two. In the exact place where our house stood, the Berlin Senate, under Ernst Reuter, erected the postModernist Philharmonic Hall. No other rebuilding took place in the area, at least before reunification of East and West Berlin in 1989, except for the church which, alone, was re-erected in all its original architectural mediocrity, marooned in a wasteland of weeds.

the large house built at Pariser Platz 1 with his growing family, but later used it to accommodate the bank he had founded. This remained there until its liquidation in 1932 and was photographed in nearly every pre-1914 panoramic postcard view of Berlin's Brandenburger Tor. The house flanking the other side of the arch was the home for many years of the German impressionist painter Max Liebermann, the only German artist of that movement to rank alongside the major figures of that particular school.[12]

By 1925, three years married to a wealthy man ten years her senior, my mother found herself caught up in a lifestyle of great luxury bordering on ostentation. This latter dimension was introduced by my father, an echo of his earlier Oxford days. It contrasted sharply with the restrained luxury preferred by his own father and mother, both of whom were undemonstrative in the reclusive enjoyment of their wealth. Our Berlin household comprised a butler (Adolf), a cook (nameless because the position was held by so many changing incumbents), a chauffeur (Frommart), a lady's maid (Erna), a Red Cross Sister (Schwester Thea), my governess, a general housemaid and a gardener.

The inclusion of the gardener was all the more eccentric for the reason that, in common with most Berlin town houses, No. 4 Matthäi-Kirchstrasse had no garden, only a large courtyard. A garden was eventually found at Rauchstrasse, about half a kilometre distant, and rented, principally for Hugo and me to play in. I do not remember my parents ever setting foot in it until my mother took up cinephotography and shot some film of us children playing there. Frommart, if not needed by Father, would drive us to the garden, with Schwester Thea in charge, and collect us at a pre-arranged time.

I am, however, anticipating events that had not yet happened. My mother was thirty-three when she became pregnant and she was determined to continue her role as society hostess for as long as possible. She was also advised by her physician to have the

---

12 Both houses referred to in Alexander's text, sitting either side of the Brandenburg Gate, were destroyed in the Second World War but were reconstructed between 1992 and 1999. Max Liebermann (1847–1935) came from a family of Berlin Jewish industrialists. (*Ed.*)

birth at home, a medical error that almost cost her her life. After a very difficult labour, during which she lost much blood, I was delivered by Caesarean section, with the anaesthetic administered in the parental bedroom, an almost inconceivable procedure by today's medical standards.

When I was finally delivered, Mother was fading fast and, at the last moment, the Berlin fire brigade arrived, having been summoned by my father, to revive her with the oxygen that saved her life. In those days in Berlin, it was quite normal for the fire brigade to render medical assistance in emergencies, particularly as it provided the only reliable mobile oxygen bank. Among the more poignant mementoes I found in my mother's papers after her death was a receipt made out to Herr Bankier Robert Oppenheim for the sum of three hundred marks, gratefully acknowledged as a donation to the fire brigade benevolent fund.

My protracted but ultimately safe arrival on 7 January 1925 brought with it a time of gifts. Father's gift to Mother was a large flawless square-cut emerald solitaire, designed specially to Father's specification (he had good taste in jewellery) by Friedlander. This Berlin firm of jewellers was renowned in the 1920s for its art deco designs, and was one of the three leading workshops in this field, the others being Chaumet in Paris and Van Cleef & Arples in New York.

Father's mother, Anna Oppenheim, widow of Grandfather Hugo, had formed a very warm relationship with Mother whom she found much more sympathetic than the aloof Lotte Simon, Father's first wife. To mark my birth, Omi, as she was called by everyone in the family, gave Mother a nine-carat solitaire diamond ring which had been one of the gifts to her from the Tsar's court before the war. The stone was set on a Fabergé gold filigree mount and resembled a sparkling knuckle-duster. Mother rarely wore it. She had elegant hands and much preferred the understated modern jewellery of the art deco epoch.

The fire brigade, as already mentioned, received three hundred marks, and the gynaecologist a huge honorarium on top of his fees, which sat oddly with his bungled performance. I was to receive a certificate from the City of Berlin, with a voucher for three marks, this being a rather quaint practice then adopted by the city senate to welcome all newborn Berlin citizens. I still have it, unredeemed. When I was baptised, some weeks later, in the Evangelical St Matthäi-Kirche, the pastor received a donation of some magnitude for the address he delivered to the three hundred guests invited for the occasion. The speech, which is also still among my papers, illustrates better than I can describe, the curious balance between the Lutheran church and its judaeo-evangelist converts.

BY 1925 THE influence of the German Jewish community, whether Orthodox or baptised, had reached its zenith in almost every sphere of public life. The banks were already well entrenched since their foundation in the mid-nineteenth century, and the larger firms, such as the Furstenbergs Berliner Handelsbank and Jacob Schiff with his Deutsche Bank, as well as the Hamburg house of MM Warburg, were joined by other Jewish financiers, among them the Bleichroeders, the Wertheims, Dreyfuss bank and that of the Oppenheims.

Elsewhere, before the 1914 war, Alfred Mond had already laid the foundations of his vast chemical combine, which developed into Monsanto before being finally absorbed by ICI. Walter Rathenau, the brilliant Jewish foreign minister of the Weimar Republic's immediate post-war years, who was assassinated by antisemitic gangsters in 1922, had formed the giant AEG cartel, and Albert Ballin had created one of the largest shipping lines in Europe. His HAPAG (Hamburg-Amerika) line competed across the North Atlantic with the British White Star and Cunard companies, as well as with its German rival, Nord Deutsche Lloyd. No example better illustrates the total identification of the German Jewish business community with the Fatherland than the suicide in 1918 of Albert Ballin, who was shamed by the abdication of the Kaiser and the final defeat of Germany. The board of directors of HAPAG named one of their new liners, built in 1924, after their founder, and one of Hitler's early spiteful antisemitic decisions was to change the ship's name to *Hansa* and to cancel the registration of the *Albert Ballin* in the Lloyds of London lists. Ironically, this liner was to carry me from Southampton to Cuxhaven on my last school holiday visit to my mother, who was then still living in Berlin, in the summer of 1938.

When studying the implementation of the Nazi anti-Jewish laws after 1933 it is important to recognise the very different effects these had in the provincial towns and in the countryside to those in Berlin. The extreme gradualism which marked their introduction in the capital reflected the different picture of Jewish influence that predominated in Berlin. Apart from the financial sector, Weimar Berlin had Jewish ownership of all the major retail distribution chains, as well as the large department stores, KaDeWe, Wertheim and Tietz being the prime examples. The Ullstein press and publishing empire not only dwarfed all the other media and printing companies but effectively controlled the mass circulation newspapers, with its popular *B.Z. am Abend*, the Berlin evening paper, enjoying a daily circulation of a million copies in a city of four million inhabitants. It was on the *B.Z.* that Lord Beaverbrook modelled his *London Evening Standard*.

Hitler was obliged to find backers to launch his own newspapers as the German quality press largely adopted a neutral stance between the main political parties. *Die Völkischer Beobachter*, the Nazi organ which had been in circulation since 1923, required urgent refinancing. This came from a number of sources. One of these was a group of antisemitic Russian émigrés, and the White Russian General Biskupsky is said to have been one of the early financial backers, whilst others were Winifred Wagner, Richard Wagner's antisemitic daughter-in-law, and Gertrud von Seidlitz, a Latvian with large interests in Finnish pulp mills. Putzi Hanfstängl,[13] the son of a renowned Munich family

---

13 Ernst 'Putzi' Hanfstängl (1887–1975) spent the First World War in the US, where he married and had a son. He took part in Hitler's failed Beer Hall putsch in 1923 and later became head of the Foreign Press Bureau in Berlin. After displeasing Hitler in 1937 he defected to Britain and, on being turned over to the US, spent the Second World War providing 'psychological insights' into the minds of the Führer and leading Nazis to the Allies. (*Ed.*)

of art publishers, also advanced loans, and further support came from Max Amann, who became the Nazi Party's publisher, having made a fortune from his publication of Hitler's *Mein Kampf*. The rabid *Der Stürmer* followed, edited by Julius Streicher,[14] one of Hitler's worst bully boys. Increasingly, in the early Thirties, when Hitler began to seek respectability among the German industrial lobby, some of the Ruhr steel barons, the Krupps, Thyssens and Stinneses, who hoped to benefit from Hitler's rearmament programme, lent further support to all branches of the Nazi propaganda machine.

Banking and commerce, therefore, were established areas of predominantly Jewish influence, but so were the arts. The theatre had, in Max Reinhardt, an impresario of genius. He had made his reputation before the First World War and in the 1920s he created some of the most important productions of the inter-war years. The cinema was another natural magnet for Jewish talent, with Georg Wilhelm Pabst and Fritz Lang as directors, and Anton Wohlbrüch (later Walbrook), Elizabeth Bergner, Peter Lorre and Conrad Veidt leading the stars. In the thriving world of Berlin cabaret and operetta, Kurt Gerron,[15] Paul Grätz, Maria Elsner,[16] Fritzi Massary[17] were among many who, after 1933, became the Gestapo's targets for their ferocious satire of the Brownshirts

---

14 Julius Streicher (1885–1946) was a prominent Nazi before the war. He participated in the Beer Hall putsch and later, as a reward for his loyalty and service, Hitler appointed him Gauleiter of the Bavarian region of Franconia, which included his home town of Nuremberg. After the war he was convicted of crimes against humanity and executed. (*Ed.*)

15 Kurt Gerron (1897–1944), a German Jewish actor and director, born in Berlin, was interned in the transit camp at Westerbork in the Netherlands before being sent to Theresienstadt concentration camp, where he ran a cabaret called *Karussell* (*Carousel*) to entertain the inmates. In 1944, Gerron was either persuaded or coerced by the Nazis into making a misleading propaganda film showing humane conditions at Theresienstadt. After shooting finished, he was deported on the camp's final transport to Auschwitz and murdered immediately on arrival. (*Ed.*)

16 Opera singer Maria Elsner made a marriage of convenience to the writer Ödön von Horváth in Vienna in 1933 in order to obtain a non-German passport. She later escaped to England where she married shipping magnate Sir John Fisher. (*Ed.*)

17 Operetta singer Fritzi Massary (1882–1969) was born Friederike Massaryk in Vienna. She converted in 1903 but was persecuted for her Jewish heritage, which led to her flight in 1932. (*Ed.*)

and the entire Nazi movement. Europe's largest film studios, the UFA at Babelsberg, were Jewish-owned and some of the classic films of the Twenties and early Thirties were produced there, including Marlene Dietrich in *Der blaue Engel* (*The Blue Angel*) and Fritz Lang's *Metropolis*. Hitler expropriated the UFA in 1934 and thereafter the studios turned out a string of banal musical comedies, many featuring the German comedy star Heinz Rühmann, a favourite of Hitler's.[18] The studios also began to make Nazi propaganda feature films, with antisemitic overtones, such as the infamous *Jew Süss*.

A rare exception was the film which Leni Riefenstahl made of the 1936 Berlin Olympic Games. She had carte blanche to create a theme of German and Aryan supremacy within the context of the Olympiad, which she accomplished with a stunning display of technical brilliance of direction and montage, well in advance of its time, and to this day studied by film students. Her film, outstanding as it is, nevertheless served as just another example of Hitler's master race propaganda, albeit one of the most seductive impressions ever created for this theory.

Music and literature were not left far behind in Jewish contributions to German culture. Friedrich 'Fritz' Kreisler had settled in Berlin, as had Artur Schnabel, Edwin Fischer, Carl Ebert, Max Rostal,[19] Kurt Weill and others, who carried on where Mahler, Berg and Schönberg had left off. Erich

---

18 Heinrich Wilhelm 'Heinz' Rühmann (1902–1994) was enormously popular with a wide range of fans. He was a favourite of both Hitler and Goebbels, but also of Anne Frank, who pasted his picture on the wall of her room in her family's hiding place in Amsterdam, where it can still be seen today. (*Ed.*)

19 Friedrich Kreisler (1875–1962) was an Austrian-born violin virtuoso and orchestral composer, whose father was Jewish. He moved to France in 1938 and later settled in the United States. Artur Schnabel (1882–1951) was an Austrian classical pianist, composer and teacher. He left Berlin in 1933 and lived for some time in England and then the US. Edwin Fischer (1886–1960), a Swiss classical pianist and conductor, had a teaching role at the Berlin Hochschule für Musik. He left Germany in 1942 to return to Switzerland. Carl Ebert (1887–1980) was a German theatre and opera producer and administrator, who lived in Turkey between 1935 and 1944. He returned to Germany after the war. Max Rostal (1905–1991), a violinist and viola player, taught at the Berlin Hochschule between 1930 and 1933. He was Austrian-born but later took British citizenship. (*Ed.*)

Kästner delighted children of all ages with his adventure story *Emil and the Detectives*, and Stefan Zweig, although resident of Vienna, was the most widely read living novelist and short story writer in the German language.[20]

---

20 To his eternal credit, Thomas Mann, a towering figure on the German literary stage, appalled by Hitler, left Germany in 1933 for Switzerland and carried on a vituperative anti-Nazi campaign for the rest of his life.

CHAPTER TWO
THE GOLDEN YEARS

THIS THEN WAS the backdrop to Berlin in the mid Twenties. My parents had a lifestyle that allowed little time for their children to share their company. My half brother Hugo, who was eight when I was born, attended a local primary school, alternating with private tuition by Mademoiselle, a rather formal Frenchwoman of indeterminate age, who was engaged to prepare Hugo for entry into the Französisches Gymnasium at the age of nine. At a later stage, I was to inherit her services for the same purpose.

In my case, life revolved around Schwester Thea, who effectively became my constant companion. Unlike the other family retainers, Schwester Thea lived with us. Her room was next to mine. My parents' suite was at the other end of the apartment, with an inter-communicating series of rooms in-between. These were, in sequence, my parents' bedroom and bathroom, Father's dressing room, Mother's boudoir, Father's study, the salon, the dining room, the butler's pantry leading off the kitchen and a utility room. On the other side of the apartment were Hugo's room, my own, Schwester Thea's, and a small room for Erna, Mother's maid.

Adolf, Frommart and Cook came in daily in the early morning from their own homes. On weekdays Father was driven to the bank around 9am by Frommart, and Mother usually spent the next hour or so telephoning friends or planning the week's menus with Cook, before getting dressed. Hugo would catch the bus to his school whilst I would be taken out in the pram, and later for walks, or to the zoo by Schwester Thea. Sometimes we went to the garden in the Rauchstrasse or, if it rained, I played in the playroom which doubled as Hugo's bedroom. When Mother was not lunching with friends she would join Schwester Thea and me for a light cold meal, either in the dining room, or more often in the playroom.

When Father came home from work he would usually spend an hour or so with us children, and especially with Hugo who, at his age, missed him more than I did. In the evenings, my parents would either entertain guests for dinner or go out, either way both dressed formally, Father in a dinner jacket and Mother in an evening gown, often in the short-skirted fashion of the late Twenties.

By the time I was two years old or so, my favourite game was to pull Father's beautifully arranged silk handkerchief out of his breast pocket when he bent down to kiss me goodnight. This never failed to send him into a petulant temper, a source of perpetual amusement to Schwester Thea, who pretended to scold me. Mother was torn between admonishing me and calming Father down, managing to achieve neither.

I need to elaborate a little on the working ways of the household. Mobility was catered for by the use of three cars, each quite distinct in style and purpose. Frommart used a Benz saloon to drive Father on his city business journeys, either to the bank or elsewhere in town. The Benz automobile company was still an independent motor manufacturer, destined to be absorbed by the German Daimler company within a few years, thereby forming Daimler-Benz AG as it still exists today,[21] whose cars carried the Mercedes marque. Benz made ugly, square but very comfortable town carriages, closer in design to horse-drawn landaus than motor cars, and not unlike the huge British Daimlers favoured by the British royal family at that time.

Mother, who in addition to her early sporting achievements, had been one of the few women motorists to pass the driving test in Berlin before the First World War, had already owned a Mercedes roadster in 1912, at the beginning of her marriage to Friedmann. She persuaded Father to buy her a Cadillac cabriolet of enormous length and huge engine capacity but with only a two-seater passenger compartment, so that I would usually end up in

21 The company is called simply Daimler AG now (2014). (*Ed.*)

the open dicky seat behind the hood. If it rained, I would be kitted out with waterproof clothing and a sou'wester. Otherwise, no concessions were made to the Oppenheim son and heir, either in terms of safety or comfort. Nevertheless I loved these outings and Mother's competent driving ensured that we were never involved in accidents.

For family motoring, other than in the city, something faster than the staid Benz or the restricted space of the Cadillac was called for. In many ways Father had been deeply impressed by his years in England, and modelled many of his personal habits on those of the British upper classes whom he had observed at Oxford. He spoke perfect unaccented English and genuinely appreciated the Victorian novels of Thackeray, Trollope and the later books of H. G. Wells, all of which he read in the original English text.

It was therefore something of a surprise that he never considered ordering a Rolls-Royce. These cars were becoming by no means rare sights in Berlin among the new wealthy business class, but Father evidently drew the line at this point of extravagance. Instead, he entered into labyrinthine negotiations with the main Packard distributors in Berlin to build a car exactly to his requirements. Packard was one of the great American marques of the inter-war years and their large saloons were often used by heads of state and diplomats; even the Prince of Wales had one in England. Father's ideas of motoring luxury were not, however, motivated by the same criteria as those which Packard's designers considered commercially best suited to the market. The car that was eventually built used an extended Packard chassis on to which an eccentrically elongated passenger body was coach built. The chauffeur's compartment was open to the sky, but as a concession, a rolling roof was fitted to keep out the worst of the weather. A glass bulkhead with a wind-down partition separated the chauffeur from the rear compartment, whilst a speaking tube was also installed for communication.

I remember quite clearly being measured, at the age of about two and a half, together with Hugo, for the positioning of our folding seats, and the exact location where the triangular cast-iron charcoal burning stoves were to be placed on the floor so that our feet would rest on them and be kept warm in winter. For the adults, similar heaters were already positioned on rollers, running on rails for easy adjustment. In 1927 modern circulatory convection heating for use in cars had, of course, not yet been invented.

The rear section of the car roof was designed to fold down in the fashion of a London taxi of those years. Father's intention was to be able to lower the roof when going to the races or to watch his favourite polo matches, so that one could sit high up on the collapsed canopy and enjoy the event with a clear view over the other parked cars.

The carrosserie was painted mustard yellow with black contrasts, and the compartment's seats were upholstered in a specially commissioned West of England wool cloth of sumptuous softness. The headlamps, engine, wheels and manufacturer's badge were all Packard, the rest of the car was pure Oppenheim. It became a conspicuous symbol of eccentricity in Berlin. There are some photographs in my possession which recapture one of those outings in the Packard, with Hugo sitting on the roof, watching an outdoor event.

If cars did not inspire Father to imitate his British mentors, the same could not be said for some of his other tastes. Every Sunday the family would sit down to a lunch of English roast rib of beef, served by Adolf in white gloves on a silver tray for Father to carve. He would ceremoniously sharpen the knife on a round steel tool and very expertly slice thin portions off the large joint, which Adolf then handed round the table.

Sunday lunches were nearly always family occasions, whenever my parents were at home. Sometimes Father's sisters or cousins would be invited, so that there were often twelve or more people sitting around the extended rectangular dining-room table. Gilt-bordered menu cards embossed with the Sphinx of the Oppenheims, which had been mysteriously annexed to the family's name some time in the nineteenth century, were specially printed every week. We two children were expected to be on our best behaviour and Hugo in particular often incurred Father's wrath for lapses in table manners, another of Father's English-inspired habits on which he placed great value as an essential part of a gentleman's deportment. In this example he was, for once, on the side of the angels.

NOT EVERYONE IN Germany suffered during the great inflation of 1922–3. American speculators came to buy residential properties and commercial sites with valueless paper marks exchanged for their precious dollars at hyperbolical rates. Equally, those Germans from the professional and business community who were still in an earning situation geared to real values saw the inflation as an opportunity to purchase collectables of all kinds, pictures and antiques in particular. Early in their marriage my parents had begun to buy from Berlin dealers, their interest lying both in pictures and in furniture. Not all these acquisitions were fruitful. As can be imagined, a distorted market such as existed during the German inflation brought out its share of unscrupulous operators, and fine art dealers numbered not a few in their midst.

In the realm of furniture, Father bought mainly French Empire and Buhl pieces and, whilst a few were both genuine and of good quality, the majority were copies from the late nineteenth century, well made but not the genuine article. He acquired a set of eight Chippendale dining chairs which are thought to have come from the eighteenth-century craftsman's workshop, and then had eight identical chairs copied. Three of the old chairs came into my mother's possession, together with five of the reproductions, as part of the divorce settlement, and eventually came down to me as a wedding gift from my mother.

In choosing pictures, my parents had quite opposite tastes. His passion was for English sporting prints of which he amassed a sizeable collection; many are still in the homes of his daughters in America. These prints came mainly from London, with purchases from Agnews, Colnaghi and other reputable galleries, and with these Father was on safe ground. His collection of English prints was entirely authentic and of the highest quality.

Mother preferred twentieth-century art, especially the minor Fauve Impressionists among whom Albert Marquet[22] was her favourite artist, and she also bought several of the highly stylised compositions of noseless female groups by Marie Laurencin, a painter for whose works the Japanese were to outbid all comers at auction in the 1980s.

She also had two very good Max Liebermann landscapes and, although this German artist was well respected in the Twenties, his pictures did not fetch the same high prices as the French Impressionists. Notwithstanding that, he was superior to many of the rated French minor figures of the period. Only later, in the 1970s, did Liebermann receive the recognition that was his due, and his works began to fetch high prices. Unfortunately, Mother had parted with her two Liebermanns for trivial sums just after the end of the war, when her financial situation was under severe strain.

The modern pictures were obtained from Alfred Flechtheim's gallery,[23] the foremost modern art dealer in Berlin, whose flair for spotting new trends in modern painting and sculpture and signing up the artists to his gallery was rivalled only by Kahnweiler, Picasso's dealer in Paris. Flechtheim was more

22 Albert Marquet (1875–1947). *(Ed.)*
23 Alfred Flechtheim (1878–1937), a German Jew, was a member of the *Novembergruppe* founded in 1918 by the painter Max Pechstein. It followed the course taken by Dadaism, which saw the most extreme form of art as an instrument of revolution but used more constructive aims for the same purpose. Its members included artists from a wider circle than that of Dadaism, painting being represented by Lyonel Feininger and Emil Nolde and sculpture by Georg Kolbe and Gerhard Marcke. The *Novembergruppe* included the architects Walter Gropius and Erich Mendelsohn, whilst the art historians were represented by Paul Zucker and Wilhelm Valentiner. Flechtheim's own membership, as art dealer, combined his role as publisher of the art magazine *Der Querschnitt (The Cross-Section)*. The composers Kurt Weill and Paul Hindemith as well as the playwright Bertholt Brecht also belonged to the group. The *Novembergruppe* issued a number of manifestos clarifying their aims. These extolled 'unity and co-operation between all artists, in solidarity with the working class, as a bulwark against the corruption of the bougeoisie.'

Ed: Flechtheim left Germany in 1933 as a result of Nazi persecution and settled in London. His wife Betty remained in Germany as she had not raised enough money to pay for permission to leave. She committed suicide in 1941 after she was given notice that she would be sent to a concentration camp. Flechtheim's portrait, referred to by Alexander, is in the Staatliche Museen zu Berlin, Nationalgalerie.

than a business acquaintance. He came to our home as a guest on several occasions and I remember his tall, stooping figure and long lugubrious face and deep-set eyes very clearly. The Otto Dix full-length portrait of him, which is now internationally known, is an excellent likeness.

On occasions, my parents were obviously tricked into buying works of art that were not what they were said to be. A particular piece which was to cause my mother much anguish was a Venetian oil painting, certificated to be by Guardi.[24] The common practice of ensuring a painting's authenticity was then, as it still is, by means of a certificate of authenticity by a well-known authority, unless the provenance of the piece was so well documented as to make this unnecessary. The Guardi that my parents bought came with a certificate of authenticity by one of the foremost experts in eighteenth-century Italian painting, who had formerly been the keeper of one of Berlin's most prestigious museums and an international authority on Venetian art. The picture went to Mother when the family chattels were divided after the divorce, and hung in her various apartments in both Berlin and London for all her life, her pride and joy.

In the 1960s, Mother began to worry about her financial situation and had some of her possessions valued, in case of future needs. Whilst her modern pictures were all well regarded, and were by then quite valuable, when it came to the Guardi one expert after another expressed doubts about its authenticity. Mother refused to take their advice, pointing out that the painting had come with a certificate from an impeccable source. Only after several more rejections did Mr Martin, the Old Master expert at Christie's, who knew Mother quite well, take her into his confidence. In Germany, after the First World War, any civil servant who retired on a fixed state pension had seen the value of his income wiped out by inflation and, in order to avoid total ruin, some resorted to desperate measures. In the case of Mother's certificate, the former museum curator who had issued it, and

---

24 Italian painter Francesco Lazzaro Guardi (1712–1793) is considered to be among the last practitioners of the classic Venetian school of painting. *(Ed.)*

whose word hitherto was holy writ in the art world, saw in the sale of certificates of authenticity a means of survival. As not many genuine pieces came his way for certification, he began to issue authentications for paintings that were doubtful or period copies.

Unfortunately for Mother, her Guardi fell into the latter category. It was not a Guardi, it was not from the studio of Guardi, nor was it from the School of Guardi, it was not even from a follower of Guardi. In short, it was a rather badly executed copy by an unknown artist who probably painted it a hundred years after Guardi. This story is sad on two levels, more so, in my view, for the prostitution of an eminent academic career for the sake of survival in circumstances brought on by external forces, beside which the disappointment of a deceived collector pales into relative insignificance.

The only other example of Mother's remaining articles of value that turned out to be a fake was a large antique Chinese jade vase. She thought it was worth thousands, presumably having paid a high price for it herself, and, had it been genuine, it certainly would have been. Alas, it was only carved from soapstone and, whilst in itself very handsome, turned out to be both modern and totally valueless. When the painting and the vase eventually trickled down to me as part of Mother's estate I quickly sold both for the little they fetched. I did not want to contemplate any decorative item which had caused my mother so much disappointment.

The only member of my family who really understood art was my Grandfather Oskar Pinner. Around the turn of the century he started to put together, by shrewd purchases and through gifts from grateful patients, a collection of Old Master drawings of quite astonishing quality. He also recognised the merit of the early German Expressionists and, for insignificant outlays, obtained works by artists such as Kirchner, Pechstein, Schmidt-Rottluff, Kandinsky, Corinth, Klee and Franz Marc. Had the collection survived it would have been the envy of many specialist museums. As it was, my grandmother's entire possessions were left behind when she finally managed to escape from Frankfurt through the efforts of her sister, Helen Joseph, and her British family. She was then an old lady of seventy-eight and in 1938, the year of her emigration, things were getting very rough for Jews in the provincial cities of Germany. Her experience again points to the difference between the treatment of Jews in Berlin and those in the provinces. My mother, with the invaluable help of her loyal maid Friedl, managed to salvage a sizeable part of her possessions. She left Germany after my grandmother, who had everything confiscated, down to her wedding ring, before being allowed to leave.

Oskar Pinner's collection of pictures and drawings was sold in 1943 in an auction of Jewish property organised by the SS and presumably went to buyers from neutral countries, in all likelihood either Spain or South America, who were known to acquire confiscated property this way during the war years, at knock-down prices. All attempts after the war to trace the buyers of the goods ended in failure.

EVERY FAMILY ACCOUNT should have at least one black sheep to provide an interest element. The nearest we had to one, and really only grey rather than black, was my Great Uncle Franz Roos, the very much younger brother (by nineteen years) of my Grandmother Pinner and her British sister, Helen Joseph, both born Roos. Frank, as he was known, was an extremely good-looking man, in the English gentleman's mould, not altogether surprising since he had spent his young years, before the First World War, in the City of London. He had found employment as a stockbroker and after the statutory five years' residence, applied for, and obtained, British citizenship.[25]

When war threatened to break out in 1914, Frank returned to Germany and lived alternately with my grandmother in Frankfurt and with friends in Berlin. As he was now an enemy alien he

---

25 Franz Roos (born 1875) is found on the 1911 census for England living in an apartment block at 30–32 Langham Street, Marylebone, west London. He was described as a Member of the Stock Exchange and a citizen of Germany. Ten years previously he was living at 101 Greencroft Gardens in West Hampstead, London, a stone's throw from the apartment his aunt Erna Pinner was to inhabit for many years after World War II. *(Ed.)*

was nearly interned but, due to his German birth, managed to avoid this fate. He did, however, forfeit his British citizenship, something which almost led to him being interned again, as an enemy alien, this time on the other side, when he lived in London in 1940 as a refugee from the Nazis.

Once again, Frank evaded internment by resorting to unorthodox but highly effective measures. He went through an express marriage with his long-standing lady friend, the very talented sculptor Loni Pickard,[26] who was German-born but was now a naturalised Briton. He left the decision to the last moment, no doubt wishing to preserve his life-long, but certainly not celibate, bachelorhood. Literally twenty-four hours before the internment order to report for transportation to the Isle of Man was due to take effect, Frank and Loni were married by special licence in Hampstead Town Hall in north London, to the great relief of the family.

When I was about three years old, in 1928, Frank had been employed by my father in the bank in Berlin and lived there in his own bachelor flat. He was in great demand by members of the opposite sex and we never knew exactly who his current escort was from month to month, nor how to address them when he regularly brought the latest holder of the office to Sunday lunch.

Frank had raised indolence to an art form. He would infuriate my father by arriving at the bank around midday, early rising not being one of his habits, and saunter into his office asking if there was anything new in *The Times*. This paper, as many others, was regularly delivered in Berlin on the same morning as in London, by means of a special early edition which was sent via the night boat to Hook of Holland and went on sale in Berlin by 11am on the day of publication. Sixty-five years later, this sort of service is no longer guaranteed, and despite all the advances in printing and transport, it is usually not until late afternoon that *The Times* can be bought on the Continent, and then only in some capitals of Europe.[27]

26 Born Leonie Martha Pickardt. *(Ed.)*
27 This was the case when Alexander Oldham wrote this memoir in 1992, but has changed with the introduction of digital print processes and the internet. *(Ed.)*

It amply illustrates the late City journalist Patrick Hutber's dictum 'Improvement means deterioration.'

By about 3pm Frank would have done a few deals with clients of the bank and then resumed his life of undemanding pleasure. He used to appear at our home quite regularly, something to which I looked forward enormously. Frank had great natural charm, beautiful manners and a very kind heart, none of which prevented him from driving some of his female admirers to despair and, in one sad case, to suicide.

He was known by us children as Onkel Wulle-Wull. This invention came from Frank's one and only real talent, other than attracting members of the opposite sex. He was a marvellous imitator of sounds and voices. He would sit me on his knee and bark in the tone of all manner of dogs, from yapping terriers to the deep basso of a St Bernard. He would then ask Schwester Thea, who adored him, if there was anything left over from lunch. As no one would remotely consider giving Frank some real leftovers, it usually meant that a proper meal was assembled for him, even if it might by then be four o'clock in the afternoon. Such was his charm that nobody minded and, if anything, Frank's little refreshments were prepared with more care than often was the case for the family's regular meals.

When I was a refugee schoolboy in England in 1938, and my mother was still prevented from leaving Berlin, Frank, who by that time had re-settled in London, was again working in the City as a part-time stockbroker, in the same desultory fashion as was his wont thirty years earlier. He was unfailingly kind to me at a time when I needed moral support and helped me to adjust to my new life in a strange country. He took me to lunch at his City clubs where I was astonished by the great number of friends he had, all of whom seemed genuinely fond of him. He outraged my great-aunt Helen Joseph, in whose house he enjoyed constant hospitality, by teaching me idiomatic words and phrases of which she profoundly disapproved but which later stood me in good stead at my prep school, where my English vocabulary seemed to consist almost entirely of dubious slang and swearwords learned from Frank. This greatly impressed the boys, if not the masters, with whom, for want of anything better, I communicated mainly in French during my first term, this being our only common language until I had learned enough English to cope with everyday life. Under such pressures this process was remarkably quick and only one year later I sat and passed, without difficulty, my Common Entrance exam for entry into public school, all of which was of course set in English.

Frank and Loni found great happiness in their married life, and Frank lived in contented comfort, his every need lovingly cared for by Loni, to a serene old age. His turbulent bachelorhood had passed, in the evening of his days, into the calm waters of a loving partnership, which for all its unusual beginnings, ended by bringing both Frank and Loni the happiness that neither had managed to capture in the prime of their lives.[28]

ADULTS' RECOLLECTIONS of childhood memories are oddly selective. Whilst the pattern of the wallpaper in my room at my grandmother's country house is still vividly imprinted on my mind (wispy orange fern leaves on a beige background) I can remember little now of my earliest years, aged two, on Omi's estate.[29] Rehnitz was the Oppenheims' rural retreat, situated in the Mark Brandenburg, some twenty miles east of the river Oder, near the market town of Küstrin. Grandfather Hugo had bought the property before the First World War as an escape from Berlin and to please my grandmother, who hated city life.[30]

It was a large estate with forests and farms, and even incorporated a small village within its boundaries. The main residence was a two-storey, rectangular Schloss dating from the early part of the nineteenth century, spaciously laid out around an enclosed courtyard. One of the memories I have is of the guest

---

28 Frank died in 1965, Loni in 1985. *(Ed.)*

29 Omi is a German familiar term for grandmother. *(Ed.)*

30 The Oppenheims bought the estate in 1905 and during the following years they restructured the farm. After Hugo's death in 1921, his heirs sold a part of the estate and, in 1931, after Hugo's widow Anna had died, the rest. *(Ed.)*.

rooms, of which there were at least twelve, and each named after a different wild animal, a quirk of Omi's. An oval, porcelain plaque was affixed to the outside of the heavy black mahogany doors, painted with the head of the particular beast which lent its name to the room. It was Omi's practice to allocate the same room to members of the family's inner circle on each of their visits, so that Father's niece Annie Petersen would always be in the Elephant Room, and Mother's Uncle Frank would never sleep anywhere other than in the Zebra Room. Only Hugo and I, and our parents, were exempt from this strange house rule; our rooms were unidentified.

The farm outbuildings were quite close to the main house and every morning I would wake to the sound of geese hissing and cows shuffling as they were led out from their enclosed quarters across the cobblestone yard. Rehnitz's farms were equipped with modern machinery and were very much run on commercial lines. Even as early as 1927 mechanical hay balers and powered grain elevators were in use. Omi left the management of the farms and forests to an estate manager and two foresters. When Father came on one of his rare visits he concentrated mainly on the horses. Friendly polo matches were arranged with other local riding establishments and regimental teams quartered nearby. My mother, never a natural rider despite her other sporting talents, managed to achieve a certain nervous competence on her two mares, whilst Hugo had his own pony. I was too small for all this but Father often held me up in the saddle of his favourite hunter, a chestnut bay called Corso.

The park contained a large deer enclosure with a protected red deer herd. These animals were so tame that one of my early pleasures was to be taken to the perimeter fence in the late afternoon and allowed to feed the does that came trotting up to take lumps of sugar or pieces of bread from my outstretched hand. One enormous stag, with magnificent antlers, was known as Hans-Hans. He would ignore all calls until his own name was called, when he would approach with great caution; otherwise he remained aloof from the rest of the herd.

Omi increasingly made Rehnitz her home after the death of her husband in 1921, only using her Berlin house for infrequent visits and, in her later years, for the winter months. She looked and dressed rather like Queen Victoria in her old age, except that her gowns were usually white or some other light colour, trimmed with contrasting bands and ribbons. She was always accompanied by her dachshund Fritz, a bad-tempered little dog who bit everyone more or less at random, and her old German pointer Rolf, who became my best friend and companion.

The journey from Berlin to Rehnitz in the mid 1920s was something of an expedition. Long-distance motoring was not yet considered a suitable form of travel, partly because the roads were generally badly surfaced but also because cars, no matter how grand, tended to break down quite frequently. The pattern usually was for Frommart to take the Packard ahead with the luggage, whilst the gardener, who also drove on occasions, would take Mother, Hugo and me to the Ost Bahnhof, then known as the Schlesischer Bahnhof, to catch the train as far as Frankfurt an der Oder. There we would change trains for the district town of Küstrin and then once more to a single-track branch line which meandered through the fields and villages of the eastern Mark Brandenburg. Our destination was Soldin, not quite large enough to be called a town but bigger than a village. It is no use looking for these names on a post-war map of Germany. The land east of the Oder was ceded to Poland and all the towns and villages had their names changed into Polish. Küstrin is now Kostrzyn; what Soldin, or for that matter Rehnitz, became I have never managed to discover.[31]

When the party arrived in Soldin, after a journey of some four hours or more, although the distance was only just over a hundred and fifty kilometres from Berlin, it was met by a landau drawn by two of Omi's dappled greys, driven by the under-forester. A horse-drawn barouche was also waiting to pick up Schwester Thea and Mother's maid Erna, as well as any personal luggage

---

31 Soldin is now Mysliborz in Poland; Rehnitz is Renice. (*Ed.*)

that had come with us on the train. Motorcars were normally avoided as much as possible and usually confined to collecting and delivering house guests.

There was a large natural lake in the grounds and boating and swimming were some of the main summer leisure pursuits, along with tennis and riding. All these activities were outdoor events, and it is for its summer memories that I best remember Rehnitz. As far as I can recollect we never went there in the winter. The temperatures on the East German plain dropped far below zero for most of the winter months, so that even Omi then abandoned Rehnitz for the more temperate climate of Berlin.

Father used to come and go but it was rarely with us. His interests were mainly riding and polo so that his visits usually meant an influx of people for the gymkhanas and polo matches that were organised.

Rehnitz was one of the first of the family assets to be sold after Omi's death in 1931, when the bank was increasingly caught up in the wake of the collapse of the Vienna Kreditanstalt earlier that year. This failure had a domino effect on the entire German financial sector and not only caused the demise of the greater part of the German private banking establishment, but spawned collapses in Paris and London, as well as uncovering huge scandals, such as those of Clarence Hatry in London and Ivar Krüger in Sweden.[32]

My memories of Rehnitz are hazy but warm. Hugo, being seven years older, looked back on his days there as the happiest of his childhood. My parents usually came to stay with Omi for a few days whilst we children would remain at Rehnitz with Schwester Thea. For their own holidays my parents tended to visit various

32 Hatry was a company promoter, financier, bookseller and publisher. The fall of the Hatry group in September 1929 is credited as a contributing factor to the Wall Street Crash of 1929. Krüger built a global empire based on match production and finance. He used an Enron-style technique whereby his businesses reported profits when there were none and paid out dividends by attracting new investment and looting newly acquired companies. Alexander's chronology appears to be inaccurate here, as he attributes these scandals to the collapse of the Vienna Kreditanstalt in May 1931, although they occurred before this date. (*Ed.*)

fashionable European resorts, such as Biarritz or Gstaad. They would invariably take the international sleeping car expresses which, in those days, criss-crossed Europe with regular services, providing great comfort of travel. Unless they spent any length of time in a foreign city where their car was not needed, Frommart was dispatched a day or two in advance, with the Packard loaded onto a flatcar, to a railhead near to the resort, to be ready to pick up my parents on arrival and drive them to their hotel, and then have the car at their disposal.

He would also be carrying most of the luggage, except for the overnight cases that my parents took with them in their sleeper compartment. This normally worked perfectly well, except on one notable occasion, when Frommart broke down somewhere in south-west France. In Biarritz, meanwhile, an anxious pageboy despatched by the Grand Hotel Palais was standing on the platform with a large hotel blackboard, carrying the message: 'Avis à M. & Mme. Robert Oppenheim, passagiers arrivent de Paris.' An envelope, embossed with the hotel crest, was pinned to the board and contained the compliments of the manager and the news of Frommart's breakdown. My parents were escorted to the hotel limousine which the manager had sent to collect them. They settled in, expecting Frommart and the car with the luggage to arrive either the next, or at worst, the following day. When he had not managed to obtain the necessary parts for the Packard by the third day, Father told him by telephone to have the luggage sent by train to the Ritz in Paris and to make his way there as and when the car was repaired.

My father, never a patient man and finding himself marooned in some French backwater, was irritated by having with him only two of his favourite Jermyn Street striped shirts (he disdained using hotel laundry services so the other twenty-four with which he always travelled were with Frommart). Thus he decided to reserve by telegram a suite at the Ritz, where he was well known. On the fourth evening after their arrival, my parents left Biarritz on the Paris sleeper, descending the following morning at the Ritz, where, to everyone's relief, the rerouted luggage had already arrived.

Somewhat mollified, they spent the day telephoning friends and business contacts and in the evening went out to dinner in Paris, properly dressed for the occasion for the first time since they had left Berlin five days earlier. No doubt the time was pleasantly spent and late that night they finally settled down to get some sleep. As they were lying in the dark Father heard a ticking noise which disturbed him just as he was about to drop off, clicking at lengthy but regular intervals. Father got up to trace the location of the sound which appeared to be coming from the wall opposite the bed – an electric clock, set into the wall just below the ceiling cornice. The minute hand moved in a small jump exactly every sixty seconds, causing the mechanism inside the clock to make the ticking noise.

Father was furious. After all the frustrations of the previous five days, here he was, in the best hotel in Paris, unable to get any sleep, He climbed on to a chair and with his nail scissors severed the short strand of electric wire which was protruding from the base of the clock and which threaded back into a small aperture in the wall. The clock stopped, as did the noise. Father went back to bed and enjoyed what was left of the night in the slumber of the just.

The next morning breakfast was wheeled into the sitting room of the suite and, when my parents were occupied with this, a discreet knock at the door admitted the duty house manager, who asked to speak to Father in private. The maid, who was making the beds when my parents were breakfasting next door, had noticed the severed wires of the clock and had reported it. The staff had apparently been alerted by the night manager to find the source of the electric failure, as soon as this could be done without inconveniencing the guests. By cutting the wires in his room, Father had immobilised every clock in the Ritz; the timing installation, which had only recently been completed, had been wired in a continuous circuit, so that one break would cause the entire system to fail. The management was not amused and, as far as I know, my parents thereafter always used Le Meurice on their subsequent visits to Paris. Only after the divorce did Mother stay at the Ritz on one occasion, this time on her own, and was received as a welcome and long-absent guest.

THE BERLIN OF the late Twenties, with its decadence and political agitations, so graphically described in Christopher Isherwood's novels and Kurt Weill's songs, made little impact on the lives of the prosperous residents of the Tiergartenviertel. Street demonstrations took place in the working-class districts of and Kreuzberg and only rarely would a really large rally come as far west as the Potsdamer Platz, which was the closest area to our apartment where there were large shops, restaurants and theatres.

The Potsdamer Platz was a major focal point of places of entertainment and one of its landmarks was the Café Haus Vaterland. This was a vast restaurant theatre, incorporating an enormous open stage where, daily, two performances were given, mainly of variety acts, dance troupes and popular musical numbers. As a final coup de théâtre, a simulated rainstorm cascaded down onto an elaborate panoramic set, with rivers and moving boats, trains going in and out of tunnels, and cars and trucks passing each other along the ribboned roads. When the show's climax approached, the house lights dimmed and torrential showers, accompanied by sheets of lightning and rolling thunderclaps, enveloped the stage for some minutes, until, just as in Beethoven's pastoral symphony, the storm abated and the landscape reverted to its tranquil calm. For a boy of four it was pure magic.

Another lasting memory is the appearance of the giant airship *Graf Zeppelin* in the skies above Berlin every other Thursday afternoon, either on its outward or incoming flight between Berlin and Rio de Janeiro. Between 1928 and 1937 this huge machine, which dwarfs anything flying today, plied a regular and punctual service on the seven-day trip between Germany and Brazil. The flights were of immense propaganda value to German prestige abroad and, after 1933, the Nazis were not slow to exploit them for their own purposes.

Although the *Graf Zeppelin* had maintained a regular service between Berlin and Rio for nine years without mishap, the Germans were well aware that the operation was potentially fraught with danger. The lifting agent in the ship's gasbags was hydrogen, a highly flammable gas. America had developed a gas which had ninety-five per cent of the buoyancy of hydrogen but which was totally inert and consequently non-flammable. This gas came from drillings near the oil fields of Kansas and Utah and was given the name helium.

Germany made great efforts to obtain supplies of helium for its airships and, partly in the hope of persuading the US to lift its restrictions on the supply of helium, Germany built an even larger craft than the *Graf Zeppelin*, to operate on the North Atlantic service to the United States. This was the *Hindenburg*, an airship seven hundred and eighty feet in length and, in 1936, pending the outcome of US deliberations on the export of helium, Germany inaugurated the flights across the North Atlantic using hydrogen gas. The Roosevelt administration, however, alarmed by reports of German rearmament, refused to grant export licences for helium, placing it on the list of strategic defence materials. The Germans had no choice but to continue using hydrogen in the *Hindenburg*, with fatal consequences.

On 6 May 1937 the *Hindenburg* was approaching the docking tower at its American base in Lakehurst, New Jersey after crossing the Atlantic. The weather conditions were unusually humid and electric storms had been raging all day. When the *Hindenburg* lowered its front guy rope to the ground a spark of static electricity shot up the line from the highly charged ground surface. In less than two minutes a fireball had devoured the huge craft, with the loss of all passengers and crew.[33] The *Graf Zeppelin* was immediately withdrawn from the South Atlantic route and the twisted aluminium girders of the *Hindenburg* became the final epitaph to the accident-ridden history of commercial airship aviation.

---

33 Alexander is mistaken on the death toll. Of the ninety-seven passengers and crew on board the Hindenburg, thirty-five died. There was also one death among the ground crew. (*Ed.*)

All of this was to come, of course, and for Hugo and me, one of the great treats was to be taken to Tempelhof airfield to await the arrival and docking of the *Graf Zeppelin*. The airship was over seven hundred feet in length, and to watch its gradual descent towards the docking tower was an unforgettable sight. When the huge craft was about thirty feet from the ground, the captain released about twenty ropes on each side of the ship which were grabbed by ground handling teams lined up on the airfield. One man to each rope, they guided the *Graf Zeppelin* slowly to its mooring mast, from which it floated lazily, like some gigantic banner.

On one of these airport visits I was allowed to go up in a single-engined Junkers passenger plane which operated short flights over Berlin, lasting about twenty minutes, for the cost of five marks. The machine was an early version of the later, and much larger, three-engined Junkers 52, famous for their corrugated aluminium fuselages, and the mainstay of Lufthansa's pre-war passenger services. They were also used by the Luftwaffe for all German airborne parachute and glider operations in World War Two. When one thinks of all the safety regulations designed to protect children nowadays in cars and planes it is sobering to reflect on the confidence with which parents entrusted their offspring to the new technology of air transport, still in its relative infancy.

CHAPTER THREE
CHANGE

BY THE TIME I was four the established order of our family routine began to change. The first indications came when Hugo was sent to Salem, a boarding school founded by Dr Kurt Hahn,[34] and run on distinctly Spartan lines. After Hitler came to power Hahn came to Scotland where he established Gordonstoun and went on to alienate many traditional British educationalists with his unorthodox methods. At the same time, he evoked considerable admiration from certain powerful lobbies, later to include the Duke of Edinburgh, who as an old boy of Salem sent his sons to Gordonstoun, despite the unsuitability of the school for at least one of the young princes.[35] Hugo for his part loathed his stay at Salem and ran away so frequently that he was to become the first pupil to be expelled, thereby setting some kind of record in disproving Hahn's boast that no boy would ever be so intractable that the school could not assimilate him.

At home Father appeared less frequently in the evenings when I went to bed and Schwester Thea was obliged to invent constantly changing stories to explain his absence. The envelopes enclosing notes that my parents left lying in the hall for each other were the only contact they had. Mother appeared distracted and

---

34 Kurt Martin Hahn (1886–1974), a German educator born in Berlin of Jewish parents, studied in Oxford, Berlin, Heidelberg, Freiburg and Göttingen. Between 1920 and 1933 Hahn was headmaster of Schule Schloss Salem, a private boarding school, where he implemented his educational theories. These were based on respect for adolescents, whose innate decency and moral sense were, he believed, corrupted by society as they aged. To mitigate this, students were given opportunities for personal leadership and to see the results of their own actions. This is one reason for Hahn's strong focus on outdoor adventure. After being forced to leave Germany for speaking out against Hitler, he went to Scotland where he founded Gordonstoun School and converted to Christianity. (*Ed.*)

35 Princes Charles, Andrew and Edward went to Gordonstoun. Charles hated it and dubbed it 'Colditz in kilts.' (*Ed.*)

her visits to the playroom became rarer, whilst the outings in the Cadillac ceased altogether.

For nearly a year, between 1929 and 1930, Father had spent some part of the week in hotels, in the company of a lady who was destined to become his third wife. She, and her place in the story, needs some explanation, if only for the oddity of the relationship.

Ehrentraut von Ihlberg, as she was born, was the daughter of a Prussian military family. Her father was a senior officer in the Imperial Army and her mother a member of the minor Prussian nobility. She married, whilst still very young, Hans-Wilhelm Petersen, just after the First World War. Ehrentraut and Hans had a son, Burki (later to perish at Stalingrad). The twist in the plot arose in that Hans-Wilhelm Petersen was the son of one of Father's elder sisters, Anna Oppenheim, who had married a non-Jewish Army officer, Oberst (Colonel) Petersen. Hans-Wilhelm was therefore a nephew of Father's and Ehrentraut was his niece by marriage.

Ehrentraut was about twenty years younger than Father and had apparently met him as early as 1920 or 1921, at the time of the break-up of his marriage to Lotte Simon. Not yet married to Petersen, she reputedly set her sights on Father, only to find that his engagement to my mother put an end to her plans. She went on to marry Hans-Wilhelm in about 1921 but, as it transpired later, she never lost hope that one day she and Father might get together. How he felt about this I have no way of knowing and my mother certainly was not aware of any liaison until 1929, a year before my parents' divorce. Ehrentraut was named co-respondent in the undefended suit for adultery that Mother brought against Father in 1930 and, after a bitter settlement wrangle in the courts, the divorce was made absolute. Omi sided throughout this traumatic time with Mother against her own son and her sorrow at the outcome undoubtedly accelerated her death shortly after Father married Ehrentraut Petersen in 1931. Ehrentraut gave birth to twin girls, Roberta and Imogene, in 1932, and they settled into a much smaller and less opulent house, where Ehrentraut's son Burki also went to live when he was not with his father, Hans-Wilhelm.

Hans-Wilhelm Petersen also married again, this time a daughter of one of the members of the powerful von Ganz family who were one of the founders of the giant IG Farben chemical combine, later to become notorious for supplying Zyklon B gas to the extermination camps.[36] Hans-Wilhelm had been previously employed by Father at Hugo Oppenheim & Sohn, until his wife deserted him for Father. He was to revive his career in a most spectacular and audacious fashion.

The Nuremberg race laws had been drafted to include children of mixed Aryan and non-Aryan parents and eventually extended to those whose ancestry included just one non-Aryan great-grandparent. Hans-Wilhelm was a Mischling, i.e. of fifty per cent Jewish blood, from his Oppenheim mother, and would normally have suffered the same discriminations as any other Jew or part non-Aryan. Protected by the influential von Ganz connection, he was not only totally unmolested but, as late as 1937, when all Jewish-owned enterprises had long been sequestered or merged into non-Jewish firms, Hans-Wilhelm had the audacity to open a small bank in the heart of Berlin bearing his own name, under the nose of Hitler's finance minister, Hjalmar Schacht, cocking a snook at the entire Nazi race legislation. With his von Ganz brother-in-law as partner they not only remained open but continued to trade throughout the war until 1944, when Hans-Wilhelm left Berlin for Frankfurt where he reopened the bank. The business was not affected by any denazification problems because of Hans-Wilhelm's part-Jewish background and it carried on business in the US zone of Germany, prospering in the post-war activity.

I was to see Hans-Wilhelm again in 1954 when I was in Frankfurt on an assignment from SG Warburg & Co who were at that time my employers in London. I found him living in great comfort and contentment with his family, in a splendid house, still active in his bank. In 1964 he pulled off his greatest coup by selling the business to SG Warburg. Siegmund Warburg,

---

36 Alexander does not imply any involvement by Hans-Wilhelm's wife or her brother in this nefarious business. *(Ed.)*

expanding rapidly in London, had been looking for some time for a German subsidiary, being loath to reactivate the family firm of MM Warburg, which he and his relations had been forced to hand over to the non-Jewish banking house of Brinckmann Wirtz in 1938, under the confiscation of Jewish property decrees. HW Petersen Effektenbank became SG Warburg (Germany), and Hans-Wilhelm stayed on as honorary President of the subsidiary, living out the rest of his life in affluence, until his death in 1976.[37]

Mother's lawyers succeeded in obtaining a generous financial settlement which, theoretically, should have secured her a standard of living commensurate with her previous situation. In fact, it was something of Pyrrhic victory. The effects of the Wall Street crash had left the bank seriously overexposed and after the collapse of the Vienna Kreditanstalt in 1931 Hugo Oppenheim & Sohn became one of the many German private banks to capsize in the financial hurricane sweeping through central Europe. The firm passed into administration and Father was employed for a short time as caretaker manager to the administrator. His capital and income were severely depleted and, with the obligations of a new family, he obtained a court reduction of the original divorce settlement.

Mother had no choice but to adapt to the new situation and we moved into a smaller apartment, still near the Tiergarten, at Blumeshof 3, a pretty side street off the Lützowstrasse, and running down to the Landwehrkanal. Fortunately leases were cheap during the Depression and Mother had salvaged more than sufficient furniture and pictures from the divorce to establish herself and me, together with Schwester Thea, in a very pleasant home, in a town house converted into four apartments.

Financial realities soon caught up with us. It was no longer possible to retain Schwester Thea on a full-time basis. I was then seven and the parting was very painful, although slightly alleviated by an arrangement for Schwester Thea to come in on some afternoons and for me to visit her in her own home quite

[37] See also Jacques Attali's biography of Siegmund Warburg, *Un homme d'influence* (Fayard, 1992), pages 227, 296 and 390.

nearby. When the separation of my parents was no longer in any doubt, Schwester Thea had, with Mother's encouragement, and some financial help, provided for her eventual retirement by renting a small flat. With her pension from the Red Cross and some earnings from a Catholic charity organisation she managed to cope well enough. She survived the war in Berlin and was reunited with Mother on at least two occasions in the Fifties when Mother went back to Germany to give evidence to the restitution tribunals. I never saw Schwester Thea again.

ONE OF THE mitigating factors during this difficult period was that it coincided with my starting to go to school. This was a small establishment catering for boys and girls between the age of five and nine, and was privately owned by its headmistress, Fräulein Lorbeer.

In Germany children going to their first school were traditionally given something of a celebratory send-off to mark the occasion. In practical terms this took the form of a Tüte,[38] a large conical cardboard container whose outer surface was covered with gold or silver paper and many multi-coloured stars and cut-outs. The inner volume was filled to the brim with presents, some edible, others for school use, such as pencil boxes, paints, drawing instruments and, in those years, an example of the latest American craze to sweep across Europe – yo-yos. The child was then ceremoniously escorted to school, where the new arrivals, all clutching their Tüte, were welcomed in the playground by Fräulein Lorbeer and her staff of three or four assistants. There was intense competition among both children and parents for the most impressive Tüte and some reached such outlandish dimensions that their small bearers were totally hidden by the treasured object clutched in both arms. I am glad to be able to say that I was not one of the young nouveaux riches.

In pre-war Germany it was obligatory for primary schools to teach the Gothic script in the first two years and not until the child was absolutely fluent in its usage would he or she reach a

38 More usually Zuckertüte. (*Ed.*)

class where the Latin script was introduced, usually not before the age of seven. Even then, some of the technical state schools (Realschulen), to which some children progressed at the age of nine, continued to use Gothic writing for much of their curriculum. The more academically demanding Hochschulen and Gymnasia accepted only Latin script and the entrance examinations into such schools required total command of the Latin alphabet by the age of nine. I do not know how long German schools persisted in teaching Gothic writing to primary pupils but I believe that it may have continued until the entire German education system was radically reconstructed, mainly by the British Army Education Corps, after the end of the war in 1945. Of all the younger German generation with whom I have come into contact, I encountered only one who could read Gothic script and even then it was with some difficulty.

My mornings were spent at school – it was a half-day session only, which relieved the tension at home and enabled Mother to reorientate her life without a fractious child under her feet, whilst I was quite happy with my new friends and activities. The school was in easy walking distance and quite soon I was given a house key and made my way there and back under my own steam. In those early years Schwester Thea still came in during the afternoon so Mother was not tied to the house.

My parents had played such a peripheral role in my earlier life that I did not notice any great change in the absence of my father. This tone of our relationship was to make itself felt in later years.

IN 1931 OMI died, unreconciled with Father and heartbroken about the divorce and the impending collapse of the bank her husband had founded. Mother, now established in her new apartment, marshalled her friends around her, many of whom had been alienated by Father's snobbish attitudes. They now rallied to Mother's support, seeing her, quite correctly, as the innocent party. My life went on unchanged but, coming home from school at lunchtime, I sometimes saw, lying on the banquette in the entrance hall, strange bowler hats or Anthony Eden homburgs, and occasionally, after 1933, military caps denoting high ranks in the Army, or, more frequently, Luftwaffe units.

Of the three services, the Navy was dominated by the old World War One admirals, such as Räder and Dönitz, whilst the Army looked to the President, Field Marshal von Hindenburg, the victor of the Battle of Tannenberg in 1914, and the traditional Prussian Junker military families, for their leaders. Only the Luftwaffe, prohibited by the Versailles Treaty, but already being trained in embryo under the Weimar Republic, in the guise of flying clubs, offered opportunities to a wider spectrum of young men.

The famous World War One ace, Major Ernst Udet, who had claimed more victories in dogfights than any other German pilot barring the 'Red Baron,' Manfred Albrecht von Richthofen, himself, was the star attraction as a brilliant stunt flyer at the many air rallies that took place in the early Thirties. He was rumoured to have some Jewish blood but still rose to the rank of Generaloberst in the new Luftwaffe. Udet was killed in a mysterious flying accident shortly after Göring assumed full control of the German air force.[39] Another around whom similar racial rumours circulated was the Luftwaffe's General Milch, who became Göring's pre-war Chief of Staff. He also disappeared in strange circumstances during the early years of the Second World War.[40]

Berlin, with its tradition of sturdy individuality and cheeky disrespect for all political ideologies, was a city in which a single sophisticated Jewish lady, with a large circle of non-religious influential friends, could live free from interference, at least during the first three years of the Nazi regime. After 1936 this was to change dramatically but in 1933 Mother was not in the least concerned when the doorbell announced an SA stormtrooper, who

---

39 The 'accident' was the widely publicised official cause of Udet's death. In fact, he committed suicide by shooting himself in the head on 17 November 1941, apparently after Göring refused to accept his resignation. *(Ed.)*

40 Contrary to Alexander's recall, Erhard Milch, whose father was a pharmacist of Jewish descent, survived the war. He was tried for war crimes in 1947 and sentenced to life imprisonment in Landsburg prison. He was released in 1954 and died in Germany in 1972. *(Ed.)*

would appear every few months, not in order to arrest her but with a collecting tin for Party funds. In those early years of the Third Reich, Jews in Berlin had not yet awoken to the deadly intent of Hitler's aims and were mollified to find that the Party thought it in no way odd to canvass financial support without regard to racial niceties where money was concerned.

Mother had many friends who were foreigners living in Berlin and were therefore immune from Nazi jurisdiction. Her women friends were often in the same situation as herself and generally went undisturbed. The first time I heard Mother speak of anyone being sent to a concentration camp was quite early, in 1933, but it had no bearing on the Jewish question. I had come back from school to find Mother on the telephone in a state of great agitation. Her hairdresser, a young homosexual, had fallen foul of the Gestapo, largely because of his loose tongue in regaling his clientele with the latest Berlin anti-Nazi jokes. Someone had denounced him, and he was arrested and sent to Oranienburg, the first concentration camp built on German soil.

Mother's male friends included one particular escort who was a scion of one of the largest German Aryan engineering families: Albert von Borsig[41] was the third generation of the great August Borsig locomotive dynasty, whose railway engines dominated the Reichsbahn network and were also exported to many countries in great numbers. Borsig was a few years younger than Mother, still a bachelor, a short stocky man with a leonine head sitting oddly on his small but powerfully built frame. In profile he was extremely handsome, with masses of thick blond wavy hair above a deep brow and an acquiline nose. Later, when I started to go to the cinema and saw American films, I was startled to note a great similarity to the actor Spencer Tracy.

Mother had been introduced to the game of golf after the divorce, and met Borsig at the Berlin-Wannsee Golf

---

41 Werner J. Cahnman says that Albert von Borsig (born c. 1902) 'became a victim of the Nazis,' without giving further details (*German Jewry: Its History and Sociology : Selected Essays*. Transaction Publishers, 1989.) An August Paul Albert von Borsig became a naturalised US citizen in 1956. He died in Florida in 1993. *(Ed.)*

Club, a meeting place for the wealthy and international set. Golf was a relatively new sport in Germany and by no means one for the masses, as it was in Scotland for example. Borsig was a golf fanatic and an excellent player and through his encouragement Mother became a highly proficient player in her own right. After a while, Borsig and Mother started travelling throughout Europe, playing in mixed doubles championships, often successfully. Their greatest triumphs were in the Italian amateur open championships held each summer on the magnificent links of the Hotel Villa d'Este at Cernobbio on Lake Como. Between 1934 and 1937 they won the competition three times and were runners-up once.

Each year they returned with splendid silver trophies, which Mother kept on her bookshelves, first in Berlin and later in London. One of these prizes was in itself a testimonial to the political events of the times. In 1936 Mussolini had invaded Abyssinia and the League of Nations, after much indecision, imposed a feeble form of sanctions against Italy. One of the proscribed items was the export to Italy of precious metals, and whilst this did nothing to hinder Mussolini in his conquest of Abyssinia, he used the embargo as a ready tool for rallying the lukewarm Italians to the martial destiny he had planned for them. In Rome great cauldrons were set up in the Piazza Venezia into which Italian civilians were exhorted to cast their gold jewellery and even wedding rings, which were exchanged for ones made of steel, on the spot. The Italian nationalised film studios made newsreels – still in existence – of this event. All non-essential items previously made of gold or silver were now manufactured from substitute materials. The first prize at the Villa d'Este in 1936 was a beautifully designed cup, made of greyish-blue stainless steel, embossed with the crest of the Italian Golf Federation and the *fascisti* national emblem. Of all the trophies that were sold after my mother's death, I wish I had kept this one; it was a small piece of history.

Mother's close relationship with Borsig was not to affect me very much as she did not often meet him at home. They travelled together several months of each year, attending the golf tournaments of Europe, and clearly filled a void in each other's lives. Borsig had not yet married, and Mother was hesitant to commit herself after the experience with Father. In any event, the Nazi racial laws prohibited Aryans from marrying Jews, and Borsig would have forfeited all his family wealth and standing if he had married a Jewess, and would almost certainly have had to leave Germany. They were obviously fond of each other and for nearly five years they defied the Nazi race laws by openly associating together. Borsig had never joined the Party, despite pressure on him to do so. He despised them as a group of political thugs.

IN 1934, THEREFORE, our way of life in Berlin was still reasonably unrestricted. Mother's golf club membership continued, although in other parts of Germany Jews were banned from all mixed sporting venues. The golf professional at Berlin-Wannsee was Percy Alliss whose son Peter[42] was born in Berlin around 1932 and lived with his parents in the bungalow in the grounds of the golf club. I remember Peter Alliss making frequent appearances as a toddler whilst his father gave golf lessons. In the many television commentaries presented by Peter Alliss I have watched, I do not recall him ever mentioning his father's job in Berlin, nor the fact that he was born there. He may have referred to it in some of his books on golf, but on the whole it is not well known.

1934 saw my entry into the Französisches Gymnasium (FG).[43] This Huguenot school was founded in 1689 following the admission of French Huguenots by the Elector of Brandenburg in 1685, after the revocation of the Edict of Nantes by Louis XIV. The school catered for diplomatic families, French children living in Berlin and German families who wanted their children to have a bilingual education, with the choice of either the Abitur or the Baccalauréat at the age of eighteen. To get a place was not easy – there were interviews and entrance exams. In my case the French

---

42 Peter Alliss (born 1931), golfer, TV commentator, author and golf course designer. *(Ed.)*
43 The school is still in existence, although it has relocated to Berlin-Tiergarten. The archives were destroyed in May 1945. *(Ed.)*

I had learnt from Mademoiselle now stood me in good stead. By 1934 the Nuremberg school admission laws already barred Jewish children from entering the higher educational establishments such as the FG. There was, however, a loophole for those children whose non-Aryan fathers, provided they were of the Christian religion, had fought for Germany in front-line service during the First World War. This was the case in respect of Father's war service and there ensued an exchange of correspondence between Mother and Father, which I still have in my papers, as a result of which he sent a record of his war service and his Iron Cross citation to the Directeur of the school.

Father's depositions duly ensured my admission and I was to remain a pupil for three years until 1937, when the racial restrictions were tightened further and all German high schools and Gymnasia were instructed to expel Jewish students, with effect from the end of the Easter term of 1937. The choice for these children was an unenviable one. Either they could go to one of the few all-Jewish schools, such the Goldschmidt college in Berlin,[44] which existed for another two years before being closed, or, as in my case, they could try to emigrate to any country that would take them and complete their education in a foreign land.

In the first few years my school classes contained a wide mix of students and, because the entrance exams required fairly high standards of learning, there were few boys from active Nazi families. These tended to be concentrated in the lower-middle and working-class social groups who would not have expected to send their children to anything other than a Realschule, i.e. a type of school concentrating on vocational, rather than academic, training. We had a large contingent of foreign children from the embassies and foreign institutions based in Berlin. In my class there were also at least twelve Jewish or half-Jewish pupils of German nationality, out of a total of about thirty. Lessons were given in French for all subjects except mathematics and German

---

44 Alexander is referring to the Leonore Goldschmidt Schule, whose British curriculum proved useful to its pupils, most of whom managed to emigrate. At its peak in 1937 there were 500 students. (*Ed*.)

literature, although children opting for the Baccalauréat would be taught maths in French and study French literature instead of German. I began to feel some gratitude to Mademoiselle, whose patient preparation in teaching me a sound grasp of French vocabulary and grammar when I was young now gave me a definite advantage in following the very demanding courses.

Outside school there was a lot of homework but otherwise, with Mother often busily engaged in her social programme, Berlin became my oyster. With friends from school, I would often scrounge some extra pocket money to go to the Luna Park, a huge fairground on the outskirts of the city. One of the most popular attractions there was a very large outdoor swimming pool, equipped with a wave-making machine, so that one had the impression of swimming in a rough sea.

Berlin provided a constantly changing variety of theatrical programmes, for which I was too young, but it also had the most famous circuses, which were still immensely popular in those days and to which I was taken. The leading variety theatre, the Scala, like the Olympia in Paris and the Palladium in London, attracted the best international acts, as well as the leading dance bands of those years.

It was always exciting to be taken to a matinée at the Scala, where once I saw the great clown Grock, then in the twilight of his career.[45] On one occasion the Scala booked Jack Hylton and his band for an entire session. They set Berlin alight with their English and American popular hits, and the band was so huge that it filled the entire stage. Mother bought all the Jack Hylton records she could lay her hands on and I played them continuously on the big wind-up Elektrola gramophone. Many of the songs had titles with some reference to 'Baby this' or 'Baby that' and it was a perplexing mystery to me why English and American jazz hits made so much fuss about babies. Whilst I already spoke fluent French, I had no knowledge of English and refrains such as 'Yes sir, that's my baby, no sir, don't mean

---

45 Grock (1880–1959), a clown, composer and musician, was born Charles Adrien Wettach in Switzerland. He was at one time the most highly paid entertainer in the world. *(Ed.)*

maybe' which was one of the hot numbers or 'Broadway Babies' who went to bed at dawn, from the *Broadway Melody* films of 1936, were a puzzlement to me. I could identify more readily with Lucienne Boyer singing 'Sous les toits de Paris,' or her greatest hit, 'Parlez-moi d'amour,' both delivered in her haunting lilt, which filled my young heart with romantic dreams.

There was in Berlin at that time an English pianist playing at the swanky Hotel Eden who was more popular in Berlin than in his native England: 'Whispering' Jack Smith. His records sold in their thousands and the afternoon tea sessions at the Eden were always booked out weeks ahead when he was playing there. The other pianist who was loved by everybody was the unforgettable Charlie Kunz, with his distinctive trailing beat, immediately recognisable with the first few bars of his medleys.[46]

Mother was not a regular opera fan but she did go to concerts, either in the Philharmonic Hall or at the Kroll Opera House. The chief conductor of the Berlin Philharmonic was Wilhelm Furtwängler and, in the winter months, he conducted a regular programme, mainly of the German classical repertoire, for the subscription series. I was only once taken along to one of his Beethoven concerts and, although I was far too young to appreciate the music, the theatricality of his conducting left a lasting impression. When I saw him again in Salzburg conducting *Fidelio* in 1947, with a cast led by Kirsten Flagstad and Julius Patzak, I understood why he was acclaimed as the greatest Beethoven conductor of this century.[47]

---

46 Jack Smith's unique and intimate singing style was a result of injuries sustained in a gas attack in France during the First World War. He was American rather than English, as Alexander states, although he appeared on stage in London. He performed in Berlin in front of enthusiastically receptive audiences. He died in New York in 1951. Charlie Kunz was born in 1896 into a family of Austrian origin in Allentown, Pennsylvania. He made England his home in 1922 and died there in 1958. Two of Britain's most famous female vocalists, Vera Lynn and Dorothy Squires, were with his orchestra in the 1930s. (*Ed.*)

47 See also the reference to Furtwängler's denazification in *Berlin Days* by George Clare (Macmillan, 1989) in which Clare, born Georg Klaar in Vienna, recounted his work at the denazification bureaucracy where he was charged with weeding out former party members from the new administration; he became highly skilled in identifying lies and omissions in application forms. He died in 2009 aged 88. For more on Furtwängler see page 56.

Furtwängler incurred considerable censure for failing to make a stand against the forcible dismissal of the Berlin Philharmonic's Jewish members. When Jewish conductors, soloists and orchestra players had to leave Germany and find work abroad, many believed at the time that he should have followed the examples of Bruno Walter, Otto Klemperer and Fritz Busch, who refused to work in Germany after 1933. Instead, he was confirmed as Conductor in Chief of the Berlin Philharmonic, in succession to the Jewish conductor Erich Kleiber, who was relieved of his post. At the same time, in 1935, Richard Strauss became the first President of the Reichsmusikkammer, a political appointment. Both Strauss and Furtwängler were later accused of acquiescing to the anti-Jewish persecution of their colleagues.

After the war, Furtwängler's denazification process was in the hands of the British Control Commission in Berlin. He had expected automatic clearance and was quite unprepared for the hostility he encountered from many quarters, especially from within the musical profession. The British did not give him any priority in the denazification hearings and it was not for some time that Furtwängler was again free to resume his conducting career. The Russians tried to circumvent the British tribunal by offering Furtwängler the position of Chief Conductor of the Berlin State Orchestra in their sector of Berlin. He accepted and was flown to East Berlin in a Russian military plane which had been sent to collect him from Munich. When he arrived he found an inferior ensemble drawn from the Eastern zone of Germany, not the old Berlin Philharmonic that he had anticipated. He indignantly refused to accept the position. The controversy about his role in the Third Reich did not go away and clouded his remaining years until his death in 1954.

One of the greatest changes in our household after the divorce was the loss of the cars. They had all been sold, along with many other assets, to find the amount for the financial settlement and to pay the heavy legal fees. Mother lost her Cadillac, and Father, when I once met him shortly after the separation (he had fortnightly visiting rights), took me around the corner from our meeting place, usually a restaurant or teashop, and showed me a small car which he said was the new Baby Buick, which he had just bought. He did not keep it long, and I never saw another one quite like it.

It has been on my mind for years to write to General Motors to enquire whether Buick, then still an independent company, ever manufactured a small model in the Depression years, or whether Father had acquired something far less prestigious than a Buick, and was trying to impress me. It remains one of those tricks of memory, trivial in itself but refusing to go away.[48]

Mother, at any rate, was without a car of her own. The reduced alimony payments after 1932 were insufficient to cover the cost even of the cheapest model then on the market, the Ford Seven. One day, in 1933, Mother announced that she and I would visit Grandmother Pinner in Frankfurt, something I frequently did on my own during the school holidays, taking the train, travelling on hard wooden benches with which the third-class carriages of the Deutsche Reichsbahn were fitted out. (When I first arrived in England in 1937, I could not believe the upholstered luxury of the third-class compartments of the LNER boat train.) This journey, however, was to be different. We went down to the street where, parked at the kerbside, was a shiny dark blue Opel, with gleaming chrome headlamps and dark black rubber running boards. It was the smallest model then being built, but it was a real car and it was ours. I discovered much later that one of Mother's elderly admirers, an inoffensive businessman by the name of Birnbaum, had put up the money on some nebulous, and probably fictitious, loan arrangement. Herr Birnbaum must have been in his seventies, a widower, on whom Mother took pity and invited to tea or allowed to take her to the theatre from time to time.

We set out for Frankfurt on the old national trunk roads, before the days of the Autobahn. The car was not very reliable,

---

48 The car may have been the Marquette, built by Buick in Flint, Michigan between 1929 and 1931. Its compact design was designed to bridge the price gap between Buick and Oldsmobile. The 1930 Marquette Two Door Sedan model 30 was known as the 'Baby Buick.' *(Ed.)*

or possibly Mother, being used to a Cadillac, treated it unkindly, expecting more from it than it had to give. When we got to the outskirts of Weimar, about half way, the engine stopped at the top of a long shallow hill leading into the centre of the town. I remember freewheeling down the slope to the bottom where a policeman was standing on a small podium directing the traffic. The car rolled to a stop at his feet and despite his frantic waving for Mother to move on, the car sat tight. In the end, the exasperated officer pushed us to a nearby hotel, judging this to be the least of all evils.

On the outskirts of Berlin was an oval circuit of about ten kilometres on each of the straight tracks. This was called the Avus and was the venue for many of the German motor races of the early and mid Thirties. Unlike Brooklands or Minneapolis, the curves were not cambered, but on the straights the Mercedes and Auto Union grand prix cars racing there just before the war reached speeds in excess of 250kph (155mph), sensationally fast for the time.

When there were no races, the Avus was a toll road, open to general motor traffic but not to commercial vehicles. One of Mother's more eccentric admirers was an itinerant Romanian baron called Boris who, in the Twenties, was rumoured to have shared the affections of Magda Lupescu, King Carol's mistress whom he married in exile in Portugal in 1947. Boris had apparently been banished from Bucharest and had settled in Berlin, whose atmosphere was much to his liking. He looked slightly raffish and wore clothes which might have served as the theatrical wardrobe for Olivia Manning's character Prince Yakimov, from her *Balkan Trilogy*.[49] Boris owned an open supercharged 1932 Mercedes Grand Tourer, a type which now fetches seven-figure dollar prices when one of the few surviving examples occasionally comes up for auction. Mother was faintly embarrassed by Boris's attentions. She was by no means his only focus of interest, and sometimes

---

49 Olivia Manning's three novels, based on her experiences during the Second World War, were written between 1956 and 1964. The impoverished Prince Yakimov has nothing but his witty repartee to offer. (*Ed.*)

when he turned up, unexpected and uninvited, she would persuade him to take me out for a spin in the Mercedes, until she was ready, something he willingly did. He was, au fond, a good-natured sport.

Boris sometimes drove to the Avus where he let the car have its head. Whilst he clung to the heavy wooden steering wheel I watched hypnotised as the speedometer crept up to 100, 120, 140 and finally 158kph. The wind howled past the narrow windscreen; with the hood flat down there was nothing to hold us firmly in our seats except our stiffened backs and rigid leg muscles. I am not sure that the fun did not go out of motoring when cars closed their tops and the safety lobbies bullied everyone into wearing seatbelts.

Boris disappeared from Berlin as mysteriously as he had arrived. One day he telephoned Mother to say that he was giving up his apartment and going to Paris for a few months. He mentioned that he was sending something over which he was not taking with him and which he hoped she would like. He would not say any more but promised to write as soon as he had settled in Paris. Two days later a furniture van drew up with a Frigidaire refrigerator which the driver told Mother he had been instructed to collect from Boris's apartment and deliver to her address. Mother rang Boris to find out if this was another of his little jokes or whether he was serious. She got no reply, and went round to his house, only to be told by the portière of the block of flats that he had already left Berlin without leaving a forwarding address. We never heard from him again.

The Frigidaire made a considerable contribution to our well-being. Until then, we had an insulated ice chest with a heavy lid. This stood in the pantry and every other day the ice man would come up the back stairs carrying two huge blocks of ice wrapped in heavy burlap. He humped them through the kitchen and broke them into largish lumps which he lowered into the central compartment. The food was kept on either side and the melting ice water drained into a sump below, which was emptied every day. In 1934 domestic refrigerators were only just making their appearance on the market in Germany, and were mostly imported from America. Berlin's private electricity companies still fed both AC220 volts and DC110 volts current into the town grid, according to which district one inhabited, although the DC supply was gradually being phased out. We, however, were still connected to DC and the immediate effect of switching on the fridge was to burn out its motor. Boris had forgotten to send the transformer. Mother managed to get it repaired within a matter of days, and eccentric as it was, Boris's parting gift was one which gave her more pleasure than any piece of jewellery he might have chosen.

UNDER THE FIRST anti-Jewish measures introduced by the Nazis after their seizure of government in 1933, many professions were barred to Jews, among them most civil service and teaching posts. In the Französisches Gymnasium this did not take immediate effect, due to the difficulty of finding teachers affiliated to the Party with the necessary French qualifications. Nevertheless, some of the more senior professors were dismissed quite soon after Hitler's assumption of the Chancellorship in 1934 following the death of Hindenburg.

One day the class was confronted by a new German literature teacher who arrived in full-dress SA brown shirt uniform. He greeted us with his outstretched arm and a stentorian 'Heil Hitler.' The normal school greeting used by masters was 'Bonjour Messieurs,' whether the lesson was in German or French. There was a stunned silence and then the class replied, as one, 'Bonjour, Monsieur le Professeur,' our usual address. This test of wills between Herr Elsässer, the teacher, and the class, went on for some months, during which time he tried, but failed, to convert his colleagues to the new national form of greeting.

At some point during this stalemate, around June 1934, Elsässer stopped coming in his uniform, appearing instead in a badly-fitting dark suit, with the round NSDAP Party badge in his buttonhole. He still Heil Hitlered, but the class continued to ignore it and an uneasy truce ensued. I always wondered at the time whether the new Directeur of the Lycée, Professor Rhötig, himself a Party member but one who managed to separate politics from administrative duties, had advised Elsässer to stop wearing his SA uniform to school classes, but it was not until many years later that I discovered the true explanation.

In May 1934 the SA under the leadership of Ernst Röhm was challenging Hitler's plans to win the support of the Officer Corps by a mixture of promises and coercion. The Army's oath of loyalty was still sworn to President Hindenburg personally, and not to the Republic, nor to the Constitution. Röhm and other veteran SA leaders from the early Twenties advocated an open coup, using the two million stormtroopers of the SA to topple the generals, and to incorporate the Army into the SA, under political control, as in Russia. Hitler and Göring, who all along sought to establish their Party's power base on a legal foundation and then to replace the constitution with a one-party dictatorship at the earliest opportune moment, felt their plans to woo the Army were being jeopardised. They feared the possibility of martial law being declared by Hindenburg and him ordering the Army to suppress the SA, if the SA threatened to endanger the constitution. This would have sparked off civil war, the very last danger Hitler had in mind.

In June 1934, Hitler was persuaded by Göring, Goebbels and Himmler to give instructions to Röhm to stand down the SA for the whole month of July, ostensibly for a period of rest and recreation after their long struggle to attain power. He promised Röhm that he would address a mass rally on the first of August in Berlin. During the month of proscription, meanwhile, the SA were banned from wearing their uniforms and from staging demonstrations.

Surprisingly, Röhm swallowed the bait and went on leave himself to take a cure in Bavaria. Overnight, there was hardly a brown shirt to be seen throughout the length and breadth of Germany. The culmination of the suppression came at the weekend of the 29–30 June 1934, with a counter-coup against the SA, which came to be known as the Night of the Long Knives.

Hitler's closest henchmen, Göring, Himmler and Goebbels, using special SS cadres, plotted and executed the assassinations of Röhm, Gregor Strasser, former Chancellor General Kurt von Schleicher and his wife, and many of the leading figures of the old SA activists. They had become a serious embarrassment to Hitler's more pragmatic plans towards achieving single party dominance with the backing of the military high command. The generals were later to experience, in their turn, a similar lesson in treachery. However, for the moment, the Army was well satisfied with the turn of events and Hindenburg went so far as to thank Hitler 'for his determined action and gallant personal intervention, which nipped treason in the bud.'

The climactic events of history roll over nations in seamless fashion and often pass unremarked until whole populations are caught up in their wake. Only rarely can the individual observer look back and say: 'I was there when it happened,' and point to a personal experience which bore witness, even in microcosm, to a fundamental change of history. The audience in the Washington theatre on the night when a Confederate fanatic assassinated Abraham Lincoln[50] could not have foreseen the profound changes that this event was to have on the Civil War and the new Union, but they were nonetheless witnesses to a flashpoint in their country's development. Herr Elsässer's shabby suit in the months of June and July 1934 may not have aroused much interest at the time but with the benefit of hindsight it was a visible manifestation of political intrigue designed to change the balance of power in Europe. We schoolboys who sniggered at the teacher's discomfiture with a sense of Schadenfreude could also not have foreseen how ineluctably this banal expression of political cynicism was to affect all our lives.

Hitler did not have to wait long to reclaim his favours from the Army, and in General von Blomberg, the Defence Minister and an old ally of Hindenburg's, he found his man. The President died on 2 August 1934 and within an hour of his death it was

50   John Wilkes Booth shot President Abraham Lincoln at Ford's Theatre, Washington DC on 14 April 1865. (*Ed.*)

officially announced that the office of President would henceforth be merged with that of Chancellor, thereby installing Hitler as Head of State and Supreme Commander-in-Chief of the combined services. The same day, all serving officers and men took an oath of allegiance to the Führer, Adolf Hitler, personally – not, it should be noted, to the Constitution or the Fatherland. All this had been achieved by Hitler's mastery of the legal machinery of State and not, as advocated by Röhm, by a coup of stormtroopers. As Alan Bullock wrote: 'The Nazi revolution was complete; Hitler had become the dictator of Germany.'[51]

Meanwhile I attended the Französisches Gymnasium, now for a full day. When it was fine I walked across the Bendler Bridge spanning the Landwehrkanal and down the Bendlerstrasse, which led into the Tiergarten. The Bendlerstrasse housed the offices of the OKW, the Supreme Army headquarters, in whose courtyard in 1944 Count von Stauffenberg was shot for his part in the 20 July plot against Hitler. The street has since been renamed Stauffenbergstrasse and the OKW buildings have been converted to a museum dedicated to the German resistance movement.

The route I took through the Tiergarten came out opposite the Brandenburger Tor, near the former divide between East and West Berlin, and from there I walked across the Reichstagsplatz to the Reichstagsufer, the canal embankment on which the school building was situated. The walk took about thirty minutes, and on the way I was often accompanied by a classmate, Stefan Eisner, who lived in the Bendlerstrasse. In winter, or when it rained, I took the tram from the stop about five hundred metres from our home, at Lützowstrasse, and went as far as Potsdamer Platz where I changed to another line, which passed the Reichstagsplatz, on its way to Friederichstrasse Bahnhof, another key crossing place of the formerly divided city. The school was just a few minutes' walk from the Reichstag.

Berlin's public transport was very good. Apart from the many tram routes, double-decker buses operated (to the surprise of many English visitors who thought that this was an exclusively

---

51 *Hitler, A Study in Tyranny*, by Alan Bullock (Harper & Row, 1962). (*Ed.*)

London feature), the U-Bahn underground network was modern and reached most parts of the inner city, whilst the brand new S-Bahn catered for the suburban commuter. Schoolchildren had a Schülerpass, a season ticket for students which covered all of Berlin's public transport.

The trams, which we mostly used, usually towed one or two cars which had partitions for standing passengers at one end of the car. These were sealed off from the main seating compartment by a locked door in which a small brass hatch was fitted, through which standing passengers tendered their fare to the conductor, who remained in the main passenger compartment. We boys regularly annoyed the Schaffner (conductor) by pretending to look for money, which we neither had nor needed. The conductor rattled the sliding door to the hatch in ever-increasing fury until finally, in all innocence, we held up our passes, usually upside-down, against the glass partition. It should not be thought that loutish behaviour on public transport was a post-war phenomenon. It was thriving in pre-war Berlin and, I dare say, in other western capitals as well.

The freedom that a combination of a public transport travel pass and a relaxed parental attitude conferred on me was fully exploited. Berlin, in the mid Thirties, was a city which still retained a great deal of verve, the famous 'Berliner Luft,' despite the heavy hand of Nazi propaganda everywhere. Films in particular were very popular and, with Hollywood entering its golden age, there was no shortage of choice among some of the great American productions of the time.

There were two large cinemas, showing exclusively American films, the Marmorhaus on the Kurfürstendamm and the Gloria Palast in the Tauntzienstrasse. I remember seeing Nelson Eddy and Jeanette MacDonald in the epic *San Francisco*, one of the first Technicolor films, and so many times did I play the inevitable record Mother bought of the title song that to this day I can hum the melody and recall the opening refrain: 'San Francisco, open your golden gate, You let no stranger wait outside your door.'

CHANGE

We schoolboys queued for hours to get cheap tickets for the Marmorhaus to see Fred Astaire and Ginger Rogers in *Top Hat*, and later, *Broadway Melody of 1936*. About this time also came my first introduction to Charles Dickens, when Freddie Bartholomew was the talk of the town for his fine portrayal of David Copperfield in the film of that name. Along with these major films, we went to small fleapit cinemas, where Laurel and Hardy were firm favourites with both young and old cineastes. These two comedians were known as 'Dick und Doof,' Berlin slang loosely translated as 'Fat and Fatuous.' All the early Disney cartoons, from Mickey Mouse's *Steamboat Willie* onwards, were regular fare and almost as popular were the cavortings of Felix the Cat. In my opinion these cartoons never received the credit from film historians they deserved, for their graphic innovation and anarchic humour.

The Kurfürstendamm was the cultural opposite to the staid Unter den Linden. The Deutsche Oper was in the Linden whilst the Theater des Westens was near the Kurfürstendamm, where the modern, experimental operas of Berg and Weill were staged. The Linden also housed the Hotel Adlon, Berlin's finest, and Kempinski, the renowned café and restaurant. The Kurfürstendamm, incidentally never traduced by its ugly post-war abbreviation Ku-damm, had the best cinemas, the most elegant shops, and many of the luxurious motor car showrooms. These exhibited not only the German marques but also French Renaults and Citroëns and English Vauxhalls and Jaguars. The luxury cars such as Rolls-Royce, Cadillac and Hispano-Suiza occupied even grander premises and we would linger in front of the window displays of these magnificent machines and avidly compare notes about the latest models.

The 1930s were illustrious years for the modern motorcar. Children today would be surprised by the huge variety of marques and the interest with which each new model was greeted. Motoring was still very much in the domain of the wealthy, but everyone's aspiration was one day to have a car of one's own. For most of the working class this remained a dream, on which Hitler cynically capitalised by using his promise of a People's Car, the Volkswagen, to be paid for by weekly contributions into a special national Volkswagen savings fund over a period of five years. No car was delivered by the time war broke out and it is entirely due to the British military government in Germany that the Volkswagen factory at Wolfsburg was rebuilt after 1945. Unfortunately, as so often in history, Britain failed to retain even a minority interest in what became one of the most resounding commercial success stories of the century.

All schoolboys of that time were infected by the cult of the motorcar and the field of study was extensive. The German marques alone were numbered in their twenties, from the humble Hanomag, a forerunner of the Mini, a tiny one-cylinder tin box on huge wheels for its size, with the noise of a pile driver and a top speed of 40mph, to the gigantic eight-litre Maybach limousines, made by a firm more famous for the engines it manufactured in World War One and for the German airships that came over to bomb England. When the Versailles treaty prohibited aircraft engine manufacture, Maybach turned to the luxury car market in an attempt to compete with Mercedes and Auto-Union's Horch, but they never succeeded in that aim and their cars became rare species, rather in the same way as the Bugatti Royale.

The Americans were not slow to claim their share of the growing European car market. All the major US manufacturers exported their vehicles successfully, particularly to Germany, where they filled a niche between the cheap popular models and the expensive grand tourers turned out by Mercedes. They enjoyed a similar success in Britain, where many middle-class motorists before the war saw an American car as a keenly priced competitor to the larger home-made Humbers and Rovers. In England, General Motors bought up Vauxhall in the mid Thirties, and in Germany they acquired Opel, then the largest producer of low- to middle-priced cars. In 1936, to coincide with the Berlin Olympic Games, General Motors brought out the Opel Olympia, a small family saloon years ahead of its time in both styling and performance. Mother bought one, and at the end of the war, when

I was with the British Army temporarily attached to the Control Commission in Hanover, I 'liberated' an Opel Olympia which, after being sprayed olive green and marked with the big white star of the Allies on its bonnet, was the envy of my colleagues who had to make do with draughty and uncomfortable Jeeps.

If there was one German car which might lay claim to being a people's car, and was actually available, unlike the mirage of the Volkswagen, it was the two-stroke DKW, made by Auto-Union, whose range included such names as Wanderer, Audi and the magnificent Horch, whose supercharged roadster became Göring's personal favourite transport. The DKW's claim to fame, between 1931 and 1939, was that it was very cheap to buy and operate. The body was made of compressed wood fibres and was thus extremely light: a forerunner of the fibreglass bodies fitted to some post-war sports cars and nearly all the small cars turned out by the East Germans. The DKW's engine burned a mixture of petrol and oil, and its exhaust emitted a blue haze, whilst the sound of its engine reminded one of a Singer sewing machine. After the war, the East German motor industry revived the car's design, which became the basis of the foul-smelling, stuttering Wartburgs and Trabants of the Deutsche Demokratische Republik (East Germany) and remained in production until being consigned to the scrapheap after the reunification of Germany in 1990.

One innovation, which appeared on the Kurfürstendamm in the mid Thirties, was an early fast-food restaurant, by the name of Quick. It stood on the site now occupied by Kempinski,[52] who fled East Berlin's Unter den Linden in 1945 to reopen in the West. The Quick restaurant was the stuff of schoolboys' dreams. For one mark, inserted into a slot, you could choose from about twenty types of cold buffet items, some in Semmeln, the Berlin short version of a baguette, others arranged on cardboard plates, cold meats, Sülze (a Berlin brawn delicacy), rollmops and gherkins spiked on wooden skewers and many other tempting snacks. Whilst the food was very good, the real attraction was its method

---

52 Hotel Kempinski. The business has since expanded into a luxury international hotel chain. (*Ed.*)

of delivery. All the items were visible from the street, stacked inside a glass tower, one dish on top of the other and each with a red button near its place in the stack. You made your selection, put in the coin, pressed the button and metal arms would spring into action, whisking the plate out of its slot and then sliding it on to a metal conveyor belt which would then guide its cargo along tracks, in the fashion of a toy railway, to the delivery hatch, where it could be lifted out. The whole of this mechanical journey was visible from the pavement, and we always hoped that some of the many buttons being pressed by customers at the same time would cause a collision – but we were disappointed, the system worked to perfection. Quite possibly the restaurant was an American franchise but, if it was, the management was very discreet about its ownership.

Skating and ice hockey were very popular sports in Berlin. Before he emigrated to the US in 1936, my brother Hugo developed into a first-rate junior ice hockey player. Skaters had a wide choice of indoor and outdoor rinks and in suburban areas it was common practice to flood hard-surface tennis courts in winter and let the low temperatures of the Berlin frosts provide local tennis clubs with a lucrative source of income in their closed season.

Every spring an annual pilgrimage set out from the city for a small hamlet by the name of Werder which was famous for its many acres of fruit trees. The Werder Baumblütenfest, when all the apple trees were in full bloom, attracted thousands of inner city dwellers for a day out in the country. Berlin's newly constructed S-Bahn went all the way to Werder and at weekends entire families would detrain and picnic among the blossoming trees. Caterers laid out long tables and many hot sausage and Sauerkraut stands provided for those who had not brought their own food. Berlin's best-known beer, the eponymous Berliner Kindl, was on sale at booths set up in the orchards and a little further away a large funfair was in full swing.

Berliners went to Werder to breathe the fresh air of spring after the harsh winter and, whilst it was predominantly a working-class crowd who rubbed shoulders there, wealthier visitors came in their cars and brought their children to admire nature's beauty, all the time making sure to keep them well away from the more rowdy elements of the throng. The Werder Baumblütenfest had a uniquely Berlin flavour, a juxtaposition of city and country, caught in a fleeting embrace when, for a few hours, everyday cares were forgotten and all the world was young.

Whilst Berlin was keeping up its spirits, in the rest of Germany the Nazis' austerity programme, adopted to conserve foreign exchange needed for the rearmament drive, was already firmly established. By the autumn of 1936, after the Olympic Games had ended and the many foreign visitors departed, the population of the capital was brought into line. Although Göring's slogan 'Guns or butter' was not uttered until 1938, the conservation of vital raw materials was becoming a top priority. To reduce imports of food, Goebbels, as Propaganda Minister, was charged with popularising the Eintopfgericht, to be eaten by every German household at least once a week. This, essentially, was a meal prepared in one casserole, to be shared by the whole family, instead of the usual Vorspeise (starter), Mittagsteller or Abendbrot (main course) and Nachspeise (dessert). The food ministry published numerous Eintopf recipes and great prominence was given to the fact that the Führer, who was vegetarian, regularly enjoyed this type of meal. One could hardly tune in to the radio without having to listen to some 'personality' sharing with the listening public his or her special way of preparing an Eintopfgericht.

As far as I remember, no one in Berlin took much notice, although restaurants were required to set aside one day a week for the single course meals. Whether such establishments as Kempinski, Horchers (the famous fish restaurant) or the restaurants of the Adlon and the other grand hotels followed suit I very much doubt but have no knowledge one way or the other. Later, when the war had started and food became scarcer the Eintopf became standard fare every day of the week, except for a brief spell in the summer of 1940 when many foreign delicacies were shipped to Germany from the conquered countries of the

West. In Britain, Lord Woolton, as wartime Minister of Food, when faced with severe shortages during the height of the Battle of the Atlantic, devised similar strategies to feed the civilian population. His infamous Woolton pie, filled mainly with varieties of vegetables normally reserved for livestock fodder, is probably the most lasting example of Britain's closest brush with Hitler's Eintopfgericht.[53]

Before 1933, a rather charming Berlin custom was enacted every year, on 24 December, Weihnachtsabend, the day when children received their Christmas presents (unlike those in England, who had to wait until Christmas Day for that pleasure). Berlin's traffic police still manned many street intersections with a 'Schupo'[54] standing on a low platform, waving his arms about. Traffic lights were at that time mainly installed on large city thoroughfares, leaving policemen to direct the local traffic in residential and suburban areas. The custom in question was the presentation of a small gift, festively wrapped, by the local residents, predominantly those who owned cars and became familiar with the officer on duty nearest to their homes. Children were often taken along to deliver the parcel to the policeman while he was on point duty, and by the evening of the 24th every Schupo's podium was surrounded by dozens of little packages, a mark of appreciation and gratitude by the community to its local officer of the law for shepherding schoolchildren safely through the traffic during the year.

This harmless and spontaneous exchange of goodwill between the public and the police did not survive after 1933, when the Nazis took over the entire national charity effort and diverted it into Hitler's favourite appeal, the Reichswinterhilfe, the nationalised winter relief programme. Uniformed SA and SS collectors stood at street corners rattling their tins, and the enormous sums raised were distributed by the State in ways which remained obscure but probably ended up financing the German

---

53 Lord Woolton (Frederick James Marquis, 1883–1964), who built up the Liverpool department store Lewis's, was appointed Minister of Food by Neville Chamberlain in 1940, one of a number of ministerial appointments from outside politics. (*Ed.*)
54 Schutzpolizei.

war arsenal, just as the fund holding the millions of marks saved by working-class Germans for their Volkswagens was arbitrarily appropriated by the State in 1939 for the war effort.

Despite the changing climate, for a boy of eleven, Berlin still had much to offer, and I enjoyed a good share of the feast. During the long summer holidays Schwester Thea was often recalled to take me to the seaside. Mother usually spent part of the summer playing golf in Italy or Switzerland with Borsig and, whilst I stayed for some of the long school holidays with her in Berlin, going out to the lakes of the Havel or the lidos of the Wannsee, the actual seaside holidays were spent either on Norderney, one of the larger Friesian islands, or on the Baltic coast, where it was sunnier and the sea calmer. In the Thirties, the Baltic coastal region, apart from a few large ports like Stettin and Rostock, was still a sleepy and underdeveloped part of Germany, with fishing and dairy farming providing the main support for the rural population. In all the fishing villages one would find smokehouses made of strong timbers, their roofs partially open to the sky, where the locally-caught flounders were smoked before being hung out on long wooden staves to dry in the sun and finally packed into boxes. The pungent smell pervaded the whole village and is still quite vivid in my memory.

On Norderney my chief interest, when not bathing, was to go to the large grass field that served as the island's airstrip. Tourists were just beginning to fly from the mainland to the islands of Norderney and Sylt, one of the considerations of the passengers being the often choppy and uncomfortable three-hour crossing in a small boat, from either Bremerhaven or Cuxhaven.

I loved watching the high-winged tri-motor Fokker monoplanes arrive and take off, each carrying about ten passengers. These planes were fitted with air-cooled rotary cylinder engines burning a special high-octane fuel, similar to methanol, used in pre-war high-performance motorcycles. This gave off a quite distinctive exhaust smell, almost intoxicating in its aroma, and I used to get as close as I could to the single white rope which marked the spectators' boundary on the flying field and breathe in the headspinning fumes. Nowadays, less privileged youngsters get their kicks from sniffing glue. Plus ça change...

Looking back to those early summer seaside holidays in Germany, I am struck by the hold they exercised on my imagination, a fascination that was to evaporate completely when I came to England and was taken to seaside resorts on school outings. This preoccupation with the ocean is much more pronounced when one is brought up in an inland urbanisation. Unlike the English, none of whom live further than eighty miles from their nearest coastline, Berlin was relatively landlocked, so that a seaside holiday represented a major change of environment.

The attractions of the North Sea were, moreover, quite different from those of the Baltic. In Norderney we flew kites from windswept dunes or bathed in rough, invigorating breakers. From the lighthouse steps we would watch the great new German ocean liners *Bremen*, *Europa* and *Columbus* hugging the coast out of Cuxhaven, on their way to the English Channel and America. We knew every ship by its shape and size, using fieldglasses and little reference books which were sold on the promenade. We watched the weather signals being hoisted on the mast next to the lighthouse and always looked out for the ominous inverted black cones, forecasting gales, occasionally two in line, when storms were expected in the nearby, dangerous, Heligoland bight.

The Baltic had quite a different atmosphere but one which cast its own spell on my fascination. We generally went to Horst, a little fishing village with just one hotel and miles of golden sandy beaches. The sea was usually calm and the tides low. I had already learned to swim as part of my school's sports instruction, in an outdoor pool in Berlin, but every child who could swim aspired to become a Freischwimmer, an officially recognised test for swimming continuously for three hours. The reward was a diploma and a cloth badge, issued by the German swimming federation, a body which already existed in the days of the Weimar Republic. The successful swimmers would stitch the emblem on to their bathing costumes and thereby gain admittance to every swimming pool or beach lido without question, irrespective of age. I obtained my Freischwimmer diploma by performing a monotonous breaststroke up and down the Baltic coastline, watched over by an official from the local swimming club in a rowing boat, who kindly fed me biscuits and sips of lemonade from a straw, ignoring regulations forbidding such assistance.

The other, and now almost forgotten, pleasure was the hunt along the beach at low tide for amber. How many children today have even seen a piece of amber, let alone found one? Amber was still a desirable commodity, made into necklaces, brooches and elegant cigarette holders or, in the case of unusual shapes, polished and set into ebony or silver mounts, especially those pieces that had wasps or insects trapped inside the resinous mass. I kept a cardboard shoebox for my amber hoard and no holiday on the Baltic passed without additions to my collection.

Life on German beaches, both on the North Sea coast and on the sands of the Baltic, centered around the familiar and traditional Strandkorb, an essential piece of beach furniture without which no proper family beach party was complete. These large ungainly-looking wicker seats were designed to be occupied by two or three people sitting side by side and were enclosed in an all-enveloping canopy which could be raised or lowered to keep the occupants out of the wind whilst still enjoying the sun or the sea view. Inside, the benches and interior surfaces were snugly lined with padded cotton ticking. Not even the fiercest gale would penetrate the protective shield afforded by a strategically positioned Strandkorb. Their interwoven reeded backs were painted with bold black numbers and letters, denoting the owner of the beach concession who hired them out by the day, week or month. I have always wondered why this eminently sensible contraption has never found its way to English beaches which, if anything, are more windswept and whose visitors shiver behind makeshift canvas windbreaks, totally inadequate for all but the lightest breezes. Many of the turn-of-the-century Impressionist painters of the German school have left canvasses depicting typical beach scenes, with these ungainly yet strangely beautiful wicker seats providing a central point of their compositions.

FOREIGN RELATIONS

The Französisches Gymnasium organised foreign holidays for those of its students who were in the Unter Tertia and upwards, encompassing the age groups of eleven to eighteen. These trips were accompanied by at least two masters and the groups restricted to twenty boys. In the summer of 1936, just before the Olympic Games in Berlin, I joined one of these foreign holiday trips, the destination chosen for that particular summer being in Lithuania or, more precisely, Memelgebiet.[55] This strip of Baltic coastline was formerly part of East Prussia but was ceded to the newly formed state of Lithuania under the redrawn boundaries following Germany's defeat in the First World War. The population was mainly made up of Germans or German-speaking settlers, and we did not meet any Lithuanians until we went on an excursion to Kaunas, the capital.

Whilst waiting for the train at Kaunas railway station for our return journey, two young Hasidic Jews came onto the platform to await the train to Vilnius, the old Lithuanian capital and the seat of one of the oldest rabbinical colleges in Europe. I had never seen an Orthodox Jew in the traditional garb of the Hasidic community anywhere in Berlin, although in 1936 they probably still existed there in secluded groups, out of the public eye. Seeing these two young men in their ankle-length black coats, with their phylactery shawls just showing their fringes at the hem and their long sidelocks curling down from under the wide brims of their tall hats, brought back memories of the vile ogre figures of Jews with which the Nazi *Der Stürmer* regularly inflamed its antisemitic readers. No one in our group read *Der Stürmer* but it was impossible to live in Nazi Germany without being aware of the yellow press and its grotesque racial distortions.

The two young men briefly glanced in our direction, taking in our German conversation, and moved slowly away to the far end of the platform. As Lithuanians they had nothing to fear from Germans, yet. Still, they probably remembered tales of the Russian pogroms suffered by their parents and

---

55 The Klaipėda Region.

grandparents and were well aware of Hitler's treatment of their German co-religionists. My reaction was difficult to analyse; it was chiefly one of shock. It crossed my mind, even then, that four generations of Lutheran conversion in our family did not deflect the feeling of guilt which I experienced. The two Hasidim, probably students at one of Vilnius' yeshivas, could as well have come from a different planet to the one which I inhabited, yet in Hitler's credo we were the same enemy. The difference was that they had remained true to their ancient tradition, whereas we had buried it in order to assimilate with strange cults and so to prosper.

I was only eleven years old at the time but old enough to feel an inexplicable sense of unease, overlaid by a shadow of shame. Whilst the purpose of the holiday was mainly a seaside sojourn, the teacher in charge of our group was a historian who gave us a very interesting synopsis on the complicated historical antecedents of the country whose guests we were. Hitler had assured the western powers that he had no wish to change Germany's eastern borders or to interfere with the Polish corridor, other than achieving a road and rail link through the corridor to the sea, this to be dealt with by diplomatic means. It was 1936, two years before the Anschluss with Austria, and Hitler had no desire to stir up trouble on his eastern borders.

Germany actually signed various commercial treaties with the three Baltic republics, and at the same time concluded a non-aggression pact with Poland. Hitler maintained a correct relationship with Poland and the Baltic republics throughout most of the Thirties, seeing them as a bulwark against Stalin's Russia. The diplomatic pressure on Poland only began in the early summer of 1939 following Hitler's successes in Austria and Czechoslovakia, and it was his misreading of the Allies' resolve to come to Poland's assistance that led to war in September 1939.

In 1936 all this was still three years into the future, and visits to the towns of Memel and Danzig, a free city under the administration of the League of Nations, gave visitors like us a flavour of two German communities where no swastikas were seen. Two years later this was to change when the local Nazi parties started a campaign for reunification with Germany, aided by Goebbels' progaganda ministry. Their clamour was to cause considerable alarm, particularly in Poland but, in 1936, Hitler categorically dismissed such fears when he assured Poland's foreign minister, Colonel Beck that he was not so stupid as to risk an international incident over an insignificant 'speck on the map' (Memel).

All I remember from this holiday at the seaside is that the beaches were splendid and little used. It was a peaceful and relaxing holiday and we were very conscious of being out of the propaganda pressure cooker of the Third Reich.

The school also organised skiing holidays for small groups of students. In my last year at the Gymnasium, when it was clear that I would have to leave at the end of the Easter term of 1937, Mother let me have one last holiday with my friends, most of whom I would never see again. The school party reserved accommodation at a modest hotel some way up from Chur in the Grisons, situated in a small and remote Alpine village, which also provided the base of a good ski school.

It had been snowing heavily all the way from the German–Swiss border and the train was two hours behind schedule arriving in Chur. There we had to change to a narrow-gauge mountain line and, after some further delay, we moved off, engine wheels slipping and engaging alternately, and sparks flying from the tall funnel of the ancient locomotive, into the strengthening blizzard. As the track climbed higher and the cog wheel transmission locked into the middle rail, the train slowed to a crawl, grinding upwards through the swirling snowflakes. Every few minutes the engine stopped and the driver and fireman got out of their cab to remove the packed ice from the wheels of the front bogies of the locomotive. After two hours of this painfully slow ascent, the train came to a stop, now totally immobilised. We were still about two kilometres from the halt, a little higher up the track, where the hotel's horse-drawn sleighs had been sent to meet us. Everybody got out and, leaving our baggage and skis on the now stationary train, we started to clump through the driving snow storm, led alongside the barely visible railway track by the engine driver with a signal lamp held aloft, and our two teachers and the fireman bringing up the rear. It took three hours, in the middle of the night, before we glimpsed the lights of the hotel, agonisingly high up from the line of the railway halt, also now intermittently coming into view. By this time some of the younger boys, myself included, were having difficulty moving forward through the ever-deepening snow underfoot. The adults of the party picked us up and carried us, piggyback, for the last stretch.

The hotel, whose telephone line had been cut off by the blizzard, only knew of our fate when they saw our small column, far below. Immediately they sent out every able-bodied adult, together with the two horse sleighs, and finally met our exhausted group, with still half a kilometre of climbing ahead of us. The smallest and tiredest boys were bundled into the sleighs, others were carried by the hotel's staff and owner, and we finally bedded down, after a hearty Swiss meal for those who were not too exhausted to eat, at four o'clock in the morning, eight hours after our scheduled time of arrival.

I learned to ski on this holiday, and I learned the hard way. Ski lifts were unknown, except at the large resorts of Davos and others like it. Even there they consisted generally of gondolas which took a small group of skiers up to the higher slopes on cable-slung overhead trolleys. Individual chairlifts and trapeze hoists were not yet in use, as far as I know, and certainly not in our remote valley. We were taught to climb using the muscle-punishing herringbone technique and the Treppenschritt, a slow side step, for the steeper gradients. We learned how to cross wax our hickory ski soles for the ascent and, when reaching the top, how to rub the wax into the wood with the palm of the hand, giving the skis less friction with the piste, for the downward Schuss. Some of the boys had brought with them Norwegian seal skins, which were designed in narrow strips the exact width of the sole of the ski and were strapped on for climbing. The tiny hairs of the fur would act as a grip in the snow and one could go up in a straight line on the gentler slopes.

The instructors, who were purists, did not allow anyone to use skins during the lessons but when we were finally allowed out on our own, after two weeks' tuition, those boys who had them were much envied.

I have not skied for forty years but watching today's skiers, loaded with high tech and sitting in their chairlifts, I think I learned a different sport.

CHAPTER FOUR
DARKENING SKIES

FOR THE WHOLE of 1935 preparations were in full swing for the Berlin Olympics, to be held the following year. The games had been previously awarded to the city in 1916 but due to the war Germany had to wait another twenty years for the honour of hosting the games. Hitler used his propaganda machine to turn the Olympics into a platform for his racial superiority theories but suffered a humiliating loss of face when black athletes won twelve out of the US's twenty-four gold medals. In retrospect, it can be seen that 1936 was the last year in which life in Berlin was relatively normal for its non-Aryan population, barring certain exceptions which did not impinge on us directly.

The staging of the Olympic Games spurred on a great drive in every nationally guided sector of activity. On the railways, for instance, concerted efforts were made to match the achievements of the British railway companies, whose LNER and LMS steam locomotives were consistently breaking world speed records throughout the Thirties. On the Berlin to Hamburg line, one of the key routes of the Reichsbahn network, an experimental single car train had been operating a pilot schedule for some months, alongside the more conventional expresses. This revolutionary train was intended to cut the time of the three hundred kilometre journey to one and a half hours, by reaching speeds of up to 200kph (125mph) on straight sections of the line.

The long single car was driven by a large propeller fitted to the rear, and theoretically, if it had been given wings, the whole train might have become airborne. As it was, it often derailed on the curves, as the control of the propeller speed did not allow for sufficient flexibility. It was not available to normal passenger use and I heard that it provided a hair-raising journey for those who were invited to travel on it. Much more practically, also in the same year, a new and much more sophisticated conventionally powered train was put into service on the Berlin to Hamburg route. This was a sleek two-car train, with diesel electric engines, featuring luxurious passenger accommodation. It was introduced in time to transport the overseas visitors arriving at Cuxhaven on the transatlantic liners for the Berlin Olympics. The time of the journey was set at two hours and the train, officially named *Fliegende Hamburger*, no doubt emulating the UK's *Flying Scotsman*, covered the distance comfortably and punctually, and was a great success.

In the country as a whole, the huge investment programme in the new Autobahn network was beginning to open up new areas of Germany to motorists who suddenly found themselves able to reach the major German towns within one day's drive from Berlin. We went to visit Grandmother Pinner in Frankfurt more frequently than hitherto and in Mother's new Opel Olympia the journey from Berlin, on the continuous Autobahn to Frankfurt, could be achieved comfortably in one day.

Aviation also made huge strides in Germany in 1936. Whilst the military programme was naturally kept under a cloak of secrecy, there was no doubting that enormous efforts were exerted to match and outstrip the achievements of the other western European nations, particularly since Britain's outright victory in the Schneider Trophy airspeed races of the early Thirties.

One day I was taken to a large inland stretch of water, the exact location of which I do not now remember, to see the giant Dornier Do X flying boat. This huge machine, the largest in the world at that time, was intended to rival the Boeing Clipper flying boats which the Americans were just introducing on the Pacific route to Hawaii and later to the Far East. The Do X was a high-winged monoplane design with a cabin for over one hundred passengers slung below. It was powered by twelve engines mounted on top of its wing in six banks of twin motors, one propellor facing forwards and the other to the rear, one pulling and the other pushing. We watched it on a trial flight, and it was an agonising experience. Although the area of water was so wide that one could only just make out the opposite shore, the flying boat seemed to be speeding along the water for ever, making great bow waves and leaving clouds of spray from its propellers in its path. After a long time, although probably only three minutes in actual fact, it lifted off, and slowly banked over the distant shore line, and flew back along its take-off path at a height of about a hundred feet, before turning once more and gradually descending to make a perfect landing. The entire flight lasted only about ten minutes. I believe a few of these monsters were actually put into service for a short time but the intractable ratio problem of power to weight, which was only solved with the introduction of the jet engine into aircraft construction, eventually led to the abandonment of the Do X. Henceforth, German aircraft production concentrated entirely on land-based designs, leaving the development of the flying boat as a viable commercial form of transport to the Americans and the British.

Shortly after the end of the Olympic Games I became feverish with acute tonsillitis. I had previously been prone to similar infections, and it was decided, once I was better, to remove my tonsils. For some reason, this operation, which is now taken more seriously and also performed less frequently, was treated almost routinely and very casually in the Thirties, at least, as far as I can tell, in Berlin. I went to the specialist's surgery and sat in a reclining chair very similar to those used by dentists. The doctor administered a general anaesthetic through a facemask and scooped out the tonsils when I was unconscious. On coming round, I was given an ice cream cornet to eat, to soothe the wounds and stop any bleeding. I was then allowed to go home and, feeling thoroughly sore and miserable, went to bed with a painkilling pill the doctor had prescribed. It must have been quite powerful because I remembered nothing until I woke early the next morning to find my throat bleeding profusely and the whole top of my sheets covered in blood. Mother called the emergency ambulance service, who took me directly to the nearest hospital where I was given a blood transfusion. If I had not woken when I did things might have ended up a lot worse. Fortunately, the medical advances made during and after the war have ensured that such casual attitudes to minor operations are a thing of the past.

WITH THE DISTRACTIONS of the Olympic Games out of the way, Hitler resumed his political ambitions. Against the advice of his generals, he had already, in the spring of 1936, called the hand of the Allies by sending a token military force into the demilitarised zone of the Rhineland. If France had responded immediately, by moving in its own, superior, forces, Hitler would have had to withdraw his units in ignominy, as his generals knew only too well. However, Hitler had read the vaccillations between the French and the British politicians correctly and the German soldiers were received with tumultuous jubilation by the population of the Rhineland, after an absence of German troops for eighteen years in that territory. Even Schwester Thea, a native of Krefeld in the Ruhr, was overcome with emotion. She was a staunch Catholic and no one could have called her a Nazi sympathiser.

Following the elimination of the last of the Versailles treaty impositions relating to German sovereign territory, excepting Danzig and the Polish corridor, Hitler now turned his attention once again to the internal question of the German Jews. Mother's ability to continue leading a normal life in Berlin until the summer of 1937, playing golf, running her car, travelling abroad and using her assets as she pleased was, with hindsight, not as fortuitous as it sometimes appeared. In the first place, her close friendship with Borsig provided her with a powerful protector with whom the authorities were not prepared to tangle, at that stage having easier targets to pursue.

Another helpful influence was the acquaintance Mother had made with the Italian ambassador to Berlin, Signor Attolico.[56] He was an honorary member of the Berlin–Wannsee Golf Club, and when Mother and Borsig returned from the Villa d'Este with their trophies, Attolico attended a reception in their honour given by the club. Thereafter, both were on the invitation list of the Italian

---

56 Career diplomat Count Bernardo Attolico (1880–1942), Italy's ambassador to Germany from 1935, was deeply suspicious of the Nazis' aims and advised the Italian Minister of Foreign Affairs (and Mussolini's son-in-law), Galleazo Ciano, to break with Germany. (*Ed.*)

embassy. With Attolico's star in the ascendancy, as Mussolini's direct conduit to Hitler, he was, in the late Thirties, one of the most powerful foreign diplomats in the Third Reich, and his circle of German friends and acquaintances was presumably well known to the Gestapo and treated with kid gloves.

Lastly, the top-floor apartment of our house at Blumeshof 3 was occupied by Britain's Consul General in Berlin, 'Bobby' Newton. He was an enigmatic figure who lived alone in his large flat and, whilst perfectly friendly whenever we met him, especially in my case in the lift when I came home from school, we never had any other direct contact with him. Children were not supposed to use the lift and, in typical German fashion, access to its gate was by a special key, to stop unauthorised persons from operating it. I 'borrowed' one of Mother's duplicate keys and, despite the house portière's complaints, whenever I thought no one was watching saved myself the climb up the stairs with my heavy school satchel. Mr Newton sometimes saw me going up in the lift but, although that meant he had to wait, he never once reported me or complained to Mother. He kept himself to himself and when he was at home his large beige Buick, with its Corps Diplomatique plates, usually stood at the kerb outside the house. Unlike most car owners in Berlin, he disdained the rental of a garage space somewhere nearby and as car vandalism was unknown at that time no harm came to his car.

Whether Mr Newton's tenancy of the apartment above ours carried any weight one will never know but the sight of a diplomatic car at the entrance may well have discouraged the Gestapo from making house searches and it is not unreasonable to assume that the proximity of His Britannic Majesty's Consul General provided an element of quasi-diplomatic immunity to the house as a whole.

By the end of 1936 the harsher climate, already prevalent in the rest of Germany, finally reached Berlin. The first effect this was to have on me was that certain school recreational activities were no longer available to non-Aryan pupils. These included sports days, visits to swimming pools and team events.

My mother's relationship with Borsig also gradually came to an end and they ceased to see each other after they returned from the golf championship at Villa d'Este, for the last time, in 1937. Borsig had been repeatedly warned about the dangers to himself, his family and his business interests if he continued an open association with a Jewish woman. One cannot hold it against him that he finally bowed to this pressure. He had conducted himself with great integrity and loyalty in the face of much hostility from his own family and circle, as well as from official quarters.

I believe he married shortly before the outbreak of war but I do not know whether he survived it.[57] Many of the Borsig engineering works were situated in the eastern part of Germany and were dismantled after the war by the Russians and shipped back to the Soviet Union. In the West the name lives on today in the giant Rheinmetall–Borsig industrial combine, one of the largest concerns in Germany.

Mother had to resign from the Berlin–Wannsee Golf Club, and early in 1937 she received the first of several letters from the Directeur of the Französisches Gymnasium advising her of the increased difficulty faced by the school in retaining its Jewish pupils. The Reich's education ministry's ruling of 1935 effectively expelled non-Aryan children from all German high schools and only the French connection, coupled with the large number of students from diplomatic families, had enabled the school thus far to evade the expulsion orders. This staving-off of the inevitable became more and more risky, particularly with the increase of new, Party-indoctrinated teachers who now demanded stronger action from the Directeur, whom they accused, not without justification, of obstructing the implementation of the segregation laws. In the end he had to yield to the clamour but managed to delay the evictions until the end of the academic year, in April 1937, thereby enabling that year's Baccalauréat and Abitur candidates to sit their final examinations.

On quite a different level, my mother's family in England were becoming increasingly concerned for our safety as well

57 See footnote 41 on page 50. (*Ed*.)

as that of Grandmother Pinner, still living in Frankfurt. My aunt, Erna Pinner, the only member of the family still working professionally in Germany – as a freelance writer, illustrator and broadcaster – had her work permit rescinded at the end of 1935 and with the help of her academic friends in England, most notably Dr Julius Huxley, the then superintendent of the London Zoo and a fellow of the Royal Society, obtained a British work permit and emigrated to London early in 1936. Once there, she obtained freelance commissions from the Zoo, the BBC and London Transport for posters and illustrated booklets, which sustained her in the early years before, phoenix-like, she achieved a remarkable reincarnation of her career in England.

Erna Pinner became a legend in her own lifetime. She lived to the age of ninety-seven and died in the same small flat in West Hampstead in 1987 into which she had moved on her arrival as a refugee in 1936. In those fifty-one years she attained something of a cult status among younger German post-war writers and painters, who beat a path to her door. In her early thirties she had travelled throughout the world, writing and illustrating her own books, as well as illustrating texts by German contemporary poets, writers and zoologists. Her longest collaboration was with the poet and novelist Kasimir Edschmid[58] with whom she travelled on her far-flung expeditions, forming a personal attachment which they shared jointly and which was to last for many years. Her journeys were in the same mould as those of Freya Stark, immensely arduous and often to inaccessible places visited by few European travellers. Her South American odyssey in 1928–9, during which she traversed the whole subcontinent by train, bus, river boat, mule, horse-drawn wagon and on foot, visiting every country except British, French and Dutch Guyana, is still a source of logistical amazement to modern-day South American travel writers.

Her bibliography includes several works that have become

---

58 Edward Schmid (1890–1966), who used the pseudonym Kasimir Edschmid, was an eloquent theorist and exponent of Expressionism. The Nazi regime banned him from public speaking in 1933 and from publishing in 1941. (*Ed.*)

collectors' items, in particular her most personal travel book *Ich reise durch die Welt*[59] and *Eine Dame in Griechenland*.[60] These two works probably represent her art as writer and illustrator at the zenith of her power. Later, in her old age, Erna was always amazed and delighted when friends sent her the book auction catalogues, from which she learned of the three- and four-figure Deutschmark prices which her old, out-of-print editions fetched at contemporary Munich and Frankfurt book auctions.

Erna knew many of the leading figures from the art world before the First World War and some became her personal friends. When I was a teenage schoolboy in London, during school holidays, she employed me to correct her English spelling and grammar at the rate of ten shillings for a morning's work (driving a hard bargain). Astonishingly, she wrote in English for her UK publications, despite her highly idiosyncratic grasp of the language. Her publisher, Jonathan Cape, encouraged her in this respect and she lived to see her English books translated into German for the German market by someone else.

In her flat, before the war, one used to run into many famous personalities. Alma Mahler,[61] Gustav's widow, was an old friend who appeared regularly and, after the war, her daughter Anna Mahler, the sculptor, visited Erna regularly before settling in California. I sometimes met Oskar Kokoschka, another old copain from her Paris years before the First World War. Kokoschka had fled Vienna after the Anschluss in 1938 and settled in London. He lived almost next to Finchley Road underground station where he remained for the entire duration of the London Blitz.[62]

One day, as I was working on one of Erna's texts, he arrived

---

59 Published by E. Reiss, Berlin, 1931. (*Ed.*)

60 Published by Darmstädter Verlag, Darmstadt, 1927. (*Ed.*)

61 Alma Mahler (1879–1964) married the novelist Franz Werfel, a Jew, in 1929. They fled Austria in 1938 for France, escaping in 1941 with the help of American journalist Varian Fry. (*Ed.*)

62 Alexander is slightly mistaken here. Kokoshka left Vienna in 1934. He felt ill at ease in a city ruled by the fascist administration of Chancellor Dollfuss and, after his mother's death, went to Prague and took Czech citizenship. The Viennese authorities tried to lure him back, without success. He left Prague in 1938. (*Ed.*)

looking very glum. There had been a heavy raid the previous night and when Erna asked him what the matter was he said, very dejectedly, 'Die Regenwürmer stürtzen von den Bäumen.' This Surrealist remark is unintelligible even in its original German; the nearest one can get to the core is: 'The earthworms are tumbling out of the trees.' Erna thought he was alluding to the depression he felt about the nightly bombardment.

For most of her life, Erna was severely disabled by polio. She contracted the disease in about 1931 on one of her journeys through the Middle East. Thereafter she walked with great difficulty, using crutches, and it was with this handicap that she emigrated and rebuilt her second prolific career in England. Mercifully, her hands were not affected and her drawing remained as elegant as ever.

On her seventieth birthday she was awarded the highest civilian order of merit from the Federal Republic of Germany for her contribution to German culture. She was invited to the German embassy in London, for the investiture by President Theodor Heuss, who was coming for a state visit, but she declined on health grounds. Erna was not a person to be much impressed by such gestures and put the decoration and regalia into a drawer and never referred to it again. I was to find it under piles of old magazines and press cuttings when I had the sad task of clearing out her flat after her death. The leather case containing the medal still had the unbroken official wax seal covering the black, red and gold ribbons of the German national colours. She had never opened it.

The stories Erna used to recount about her fellow artists would have made a telling cahier d'époque. One of her oldest friends was Dr Berta Geissmar who had been Furtwängler's personal assistant. Being Jewish, she was forced out of her job despite Furtwängler's intercession on her behalf, and she came to London with a letter from Furtwängler to Sir Thomas Beecham, who employed her as his secretary, a position she retained until her retirement. Geissmar's recollections, published under the title *The Baton and the Jackboot*,[63] provide a piercing insight into the impact of the Third Reich on German musicians and conductors, some of whom behaved honorably, others far less so, towards their Jewish colleagues.[64]

Towards the end of her life Erna still maintained her robust, self-deprecating sense of humour. When anyone telephoned to ask how she was she inevitably replied, 'I'm still here.'

Erna Pinner was one of the last Central European grandes personnages littéraires of the early twentieth century. Modest, tough, unsentimental and inquisitive, she triumphed over personal adversity. Eccentric when it suited her, yet always practical and never overawed, she met life's challenges head on, and usually won. Her English pronunciation had to be heard to be believed, yet she wrote in the language with great fluency. I cherish memories of her invitations to have a little 'snake' with her.

Clothes meant nothing to her and she seldom left her home. My mother used to buy her dresses when she felt Erna's were becoming too shabby. A friend once left her an old fur coat in her will. It was unfashionable but still quite wearable and would have been very useful for Erna when she was pushed in her wheelchair for her short 'walks' in the winter. She loathed it and called it 'Ein totgekitzelter Hund.' This is a derogatory slang expression for an old fox fur, such as those which were in fashion before the war. In English it means literally 'A tickled-to-death dog.' She regularly hung it out from the ground floor window of her flat, hoping that some passer-by would steal it and she could claim on the insurance. It hung there, week in week out, in its transparent plastic mothproof zip case, until one day the cover and hanger had gone and only the coat was left hanging on a nail just below the window sill, undesired even by the thief. Erna conceded defeat and the coat went to a Jewish charity.

Erna Pinner was the only self-sufficient, independent and bountifully gifted character in our family during my lifetime. Despite her great physical disadvantages she continued to expand

63 Published by Hamish Hamilton, 1944. (*Ed.*)
64 See also pages 55–56. (*Ed.*)

the boundaries of her many talents, to a high and honourable old age. Her work encompassed the writing and illustration of worldwide travel books, the study and exploration of animal behaviour, broadcasting and freelance contributions to many international publications. Her work in the visual arts, for which she was trained, included oils and watercolours, lino and woodcuts, and above all else, a huge output of exquisite pen and ink drawings. Her bibliography extends to fifty-nine books of illustrations, including those written and illustrated by herself. Erna Pinner's mastery of sensitive animal illustrations is recognised by the inclusion of her work in the collections of museums in her native Germany and in England, her adopted country. Of all the many 'foreign relations,' now deceased, I miss her more than most.

My Grandmother Pinner's younger sister, Helene Roos, had married an English naturalised Jew, Leopold Joseph, around 1895.[65] He was a descendant from an earlier wave of immigrants who had arrived in England in the 1860s. Leopold had founded the merchant bank of Leopold Joseph & Sons in the City of London after the First World War, having previously been employed by Reuters. All the four sons born to Leopold and Helene were native Britons and, in the closing stages of the First World War, the eldest, Bertie, served in the British Army as an officer in the Honourable Artillery Company.

Helen, as she was called in England, was increasingly worried about her sister in Frankfurt and in 1936 sent Oscar and Teddy Joseph to Germany to urge her and my mother to expedite their emigration affairs and, as a matter of urgency, to bring me to London so that my education could continue after my enforced departure from the Französisches Gymnasium in April 1937. Mother was still living relatively comfortably in her apartment and had recently taken on Friedl Graupner, a young Aryan girl, as maid. Friedl was to prove herself, in the difficult years to come,

---

65 Helene and Leopold and their four sons, Albert, Henry, Stanley and Edward, along with three live-in servants, occupied a large house at 65 Compayne Gardens, West Hampstead in north-west London. (*Ed.*)

a person of outstanding character and resourcefulness to whose unflinching loyalty both my mother and I owe a lasting debt of gratitude. I was finally able to make these sentiments known to Friedl when I visited Berlin on two occasions in the 1980s. I found her alive and well, living in a tenement block dating back to the early part of the century, which had survived the destruction in Berlin. She had suffered great brutality at the hands of the invading Russian soldiers in 1945 but had rebuilt her life gradually, so that only her advancing age remained her main enemy.

ENGLAND AND THE WAR

CHAPTER FIVE
EMIGRATION

THE ATTITUDE OF the western democracies to the situation of the Jews in Germany was at best indifferent and at worst positively hostile. The famous quote attributed to a senior British civil servant responsible for a section dealing with admission visas for German Jewish refugees – 'It's always these wailing Jews' – is well documented and reflects official policy on immigration in the late Thirties. There were basically only two ways in which German Jews could obtain a British entry visa. The first was secured by a guarantee given by the applicant's British sponsor, to the effect that the immigrant would not become a burden on the State. The other route was mainly reserved for children, especially those who were already orphaned as a result of their parents' disappearance into concentration camps.

Several British–Jewish organisations sprang up and organised children's transports, rescuing many thousands before the war put a stop to these convoys.[66] Once in England, the children were found homes with foster parents, and the humane treatment by the UK authorities and the adoptive guardians of these children is one of the redeeming features of that tragic chapter.

In my case, the Joseph family, appalled by the fact-finding visit conducted by Oscar and Teddy in Germany, applied to the UK immigration authorities without delay, lodging the necessary guarantees for my grandmother, mother and myself. As a minor, I still had my German passport, whereas Mother's was confiscated as soon as my application for an exit visa was lodged. This was

---

66 Oscar Joseph, as Chairman of the Central British Fund for Refugees, played a prominent role in this rescue work, emulating the pioneering work in this field of Otto Schiff, a Jewish emigré philanthropist who had established children's homes in various parts of the UK, all financed by charitable contributions from the British Jewish community.

EMIGRATION

standard blackmail practised by the Reichsfluchtsteueramt, the taxation section responsible for the sequestration of all Jewish-owned assets, before granting an exit visa for the purpose of emigration.

Even before I was forced to leave the Französisches Gymnasium in the spring of 1937, my mother had already made a number of approaches to friends living in Switzerland, and in particular to her old school friend Martha Dreyfuss, whose husband Willy had once operated a private bank similar to that of Hugo Oppenheim & Sohn in Berlin, but who had grasped the meaning of National Socialism earlier than most and had transferred his family and his business to Switzerland before Hitler came to power. Martha Dreyfuss was my godmother and she was anxious for me to attend a Swiss boarding school and guaranteed to meet the fees, at least until such time as my mother could leave Germany and our future abode be settled. In fact, this plan would never have been anything more than a stop-gap measure as the Swiss authorities were not prepared to grant permanent residence permits, even to schoolboys.

This left the Josephs' proposal as the only realistic option, and beginning in April 1937 I was started on a crash course in English, a language totally foreign to me up to that time. Mother engaged a tutor, an English teacher living in Berlin by the name of Miss Shott, nicknamed Shottie. She came to our flat most mornings and demanded a constant supply of shortbread biscuits, without which she was apparently unable to function. Her ample figure testified to this craving and at first Mother went along with her whim. The biscuits were not available from normal grocery outlets and had to be obtained from Rollenhagen, a kind of Berlin Fauchon and the only provision store to stock such items as English breakfast marmalades, Dundee cakes, speciality teas, Kellogg's cornflakes, and all manner of Scottish shortbread confections. The experiment of learning English from Shottie was not very successful as she always had a mouth full of crumbs, and I could not follow her phonetic pronunciation. After a few weeks, during which I made virtually no progress, she was dismissed, and I did not receive any further English lessons until I actually arrived in Britain.

Mother had meanwhile obtained a four-week exit visa, secured by putting her entire assets – bank accounts, stocks and shares, furniture, jewellery, silver and paintings – in escrow to the German authorities. A carnet was officially prepared, listing every item and its value, and Mother would have forfeited everything if she had failed to return to Berlin. Even so, I think she was prepared to lose all her possessions and remain in England at the end of the four weeks but her UK entry visa had not yet been processed and she would have been deported. This left her with no alternative but to go back to Berlin at the end of the four weeks, whilst I stayed on in England.

The few months of mid-1937 must have been a nightmare for my mother. She knew that I would soon be living in England but was by no means optimistic of being allowed to follow me. One particular incident from those stressful weeks still comes to mind. I was taken ill with a rather severe form of measles, a disease which was regarded quite seriously in those days, as there was no effective treatment except lying in a darkened room waiting for the fever to subside and the rash to recede. This illness coincided with the coronation of King George VI on 12 May 1937, and Deutschlandsender, the German long wave transmitter, relayed the entire five-hour ceremony from London, including the reportage inside Westminster Abbey, taking the live broadcast from the BBC. Hitler had made friendly contacts with Edward VIII and was now anxious to re-establish good relations with the British government and the new monarchy. He encouraged the German public to take interest in a historical event in the one European country towards which his attitude remained ambivalent right up the the end of the third Reich.

I had been given Mother's old radio, which I kept in my room, and although I did not understand much of the splendid oratory, the sense of occasion left an indelible impression, one that I was to recapture when I watched the coronation of Queen Elizabeth II on television many years later. I had meanwhile received my last school report from the Französisches Gymnasium in which the reason for leaving was given as 'In order to continue his education abroad.' No mention was made of the real reasons and I have never been able to decide whether the wording was an act of kindness on the part of the Directeur or a shameless piece of hypocrisy.

In September 1937 Mother and I arrived at London's Liverpool Street station, from the overnight Hook of Holland to Harwich ferry. We took a taxi to Helen Joseph's house at 64 Compayne Gardens, West Hampstead. To this day I remember the fare – it was £1 12s. 6d. There was heavy rain in London that morning and the taxi, which had a collapsible rear roof, was cold and draughty. After about an hour's drive through the densest traffic I had ever seen, we arrived at Great Aunt Helen's house where the entire Joseph family had gathered to welcome us. Helen and Mother embraced warmly whilst the Joseph brothers, Bertie, Oscar, Stanley and Teddy, took it in turns to ply me with questions about the journey. Only Teddy spoke fluent German and he became my guardian during the long wait for Mother to make her escape from Germany, in the event not until November 1938.

I had to wait two months for the start of the next term at Falconbury School, the boarding preparatory school near Cooden Beach, Sussex selected for me by the Josephs. During my stay in London, after Mother's return to Berlin, Oscar Joseph put me up in his flat at 16 St John's Wood Park in Avenue Road, where he lived from the day he moved in, some time in 1936, until his death in 1989. As the Joseph brothers were all working in the City during the day it was left to Great Aunt Helen in the main to entertain me. The Josephs were quite affluent and kept a large Humber limousine which took Leopold to his office every morning. It was driven by a very nice chauffeur, by the name of Guntry, who was dispatched to take me to places like Richmond Park, where the deer brought back memories of our herd in Rehnitz, or to Kew Gardens, where I loved going around the great palm houses.

Occasionally, Helen would take me along on her shopping trips in the West End or Knightsbridge and we would have lunch, sometimes at Gunter's Tea Shop or Fortnum & Mason. On one occasion, in the early days of my stay in London, after Mother had gone back to Germany, Helen took me to Harrods where we went to the splendid Georgian restaurant, all dark mahogany and white linen. I was not yet accustomed to some of the typical English dishes and when I saw that there were sausages on the menu I knew what I wanted to order. Helen demurred, thinking no doubt that eating sausages in Harrods was not quite right, but she allowed me to have my way.

In Berlin sausages of all kinds were regular fare and our supper would often consist of an Aufschnitt Teller, a collation of sliced smoked sausages and other cold meats. My sausages duly arrived, beautifully presented under a silver cover, surrounded by a wavy ring of mashed potatoes. I fell on them hungrily but the first bite became one of the greatest disappointments of my, until then, sheltered life. The English sausage was so far removed from any I had ever tasted that all my pent-up feelings of homesickness were released in a flood of tears. Nothing that the attentions of the waitress, the restaurant manager and of course Helen herself could do would comfort me and we departed by taxi for Compayne Gardens, a worried and protective old English lady with a forlorn boy in tow. When we got back to the house, Helen ordered a large tea and, after toasted tea cakes and several slices of Fortnum's cakes, my spirits were gradually restored. It took me as least ten years to appreciate the finer points of the British sausage as only in the Fifties did they return to their pre-war quality and, by then and ever after, I had come to regard their better varieties as worthy equals to the panoplied arrays of Wurst that had figured so largely in my Berlin childhood.

Mother and I owed an enormous debt of gratitude to the Josephs. Our families had never been very close; they regarded my father as a rather snobbish bon viveur, whilst he made no attempt to endear himself to Mother's English side of the family. They nevertheless remained steadfast in their loyalty and support and in the final analysis we owe them nothing less than our escape from Hitler's Holocaust.

If this account makes little mention of my father after the

divorce in 1930, it is because my contact with him became more and more infrequent. Although he had obtained fortnightly visiting rights as part of the divorce settlement, in practice these did not happen. My mother's resentment of his new wife, who had been a welcome guest in our house whilst married to Father's nephew Hans-Wilhelm Petersen, was unconcealed, and her bitterness at this betrayal within the inner circle of the family had wounded her deeply. This undoubtedly rubbed off on me and affected my own relationship with Father. On the relatively rare occasions when I went to his house for Sunday lunch, the atmosphere was very strained. This estrangement intensified after the birth of Father's twin girls in 1932, and by the mid-Thirties Father and I would only see each other about half a dozen times a year.

By 1937, preoccupied with my own impending emigration, I had lost contact with Father altogether, since he had no role to play in these arrangements and was in any case unable to help. After I came to England we exchanged sporadic and unemotional letters and when war broke out in September 1939 this correspondence ceased altogether, as he was still living in Berlin.

Two years earlier, seeing no possibility of any form of employment in Germany as a non-Aryan, Father had travelled to London to see if he could find some means of reactivating his financial career and thereby extricating himself and his family from an increasingly desperate situation in Germany. This visit turned out to be a total disappointment; his contacts were too old and too remote to be of any use to him now. He returned to Berlin and, through the protection of the aristocratic relations of his Aryan wife, remained quite unmolested. However, with no income and dwindling capital, the family became more impoverished with every year that passed. Most of Father's remaining valuables, which had passed to him after the divorce from Mother, were sold off at this time. Not until May 1940, after the fall of France, and just before Italy's entry into the war on Germany's side, did his wife's von Ihlberg connections finally obtain an exit visa for him, his wife and their children. They left by train via Switzerland for the then still neutral Italy, where they boarded the Italia line flagship *Rex* at Genoa, bound for New York. It was to be the last peacetime sailing from any Italian port to the United States. By the time the ship arrived in New York, Italy had become a belligerent power and, under their Neutrality Act, the US authorities impounded the ship in New York harbour, where it remained throughout the duration of the war, finally to become part of the Italian war reparations. To say that Father and his family escaped from Germany at a minute to midnight would be an understatement. He achieved the statistically impossible by stopping the persecution clock for a whole year after the final deadline had passed. There could not have been many Jews in Germany who reached freedom as late as June 1940.

In New York Father tried once more to find a job in the financial world of Wall Street but his lack of funds and advanced age combined to frustrate his hopes. After a few months, with the advice and help of friends, many of whom had settled in America years earlier, he bought a small guest house in the ski resort of North Conway, New Hampshire. This became his family's home, in which they accommodated a few guests, mostly former acquaintances from Europe, who came up from New York to ski in the White Mountains.

After a life of extraordinary privilege and self-indulgence, Father spent the last years of his life polishing his guests' shoes after they had retired for the night and during the day entertaining them with all his Old World charm and courtesy. His wife, then still only in her late forties, worked herself to exhaustion, running the business, cooking, cleaning and supervising the casual staff, whilst raising her two children. I have little reason to give credit to the woman who effectively erected an insurmountable barrier between my father and me but I have to acknowledge her indomitable spirit in the years of adversity that befell them. Father, to his credit, accepted the situation philosophically and accounts I later received from some of his guests of those years were unanimous in the opinion that he was not embittered by his fate and that he finally found, in the company of his wife and young daughters, the sense of belonging that had eluded him in all the years when his fortunes rode high. He died in 1956 at the age of 74, followed only four years later by his wife, at the early age of 60.

I never saw my father again after 1936 and, despite all that passed between us which made our relationship so difficult, I am conscious of a great loss of a part of my formative years, for not having known him better. For this I bear at least some of the responsibility, through my own neglect of the relationship and the prejudice that accompanied it. My father had caused much unhappiness to those who were closest to him and later, when some of the wrongs of the past might have been addressed, if not resolved, it was too late; circumstances conspired against him. I realise now that my loss is one of never having known my father very well.

IN NOVEMBER 1937, when her temporary visa expired, Mother left London and returned to Berlin. We saw her off at Croydon aerodrome and when the Lufthansa Heinkel lifted off the runway, the swastika ominously large on its tailplane, reality suddenly closed in on me. A door was closing on a chapter of my life where all had been familiar; the future was something I could not think about, only the certainty that nothing would ever be the same. The strange country which had opened its doors to me was now to be my home; somehow I would learn to understand its ways. My Berlin Kinderheit receded, its shadows already lengthening. Ahead, still unimaginable, lay my English adolescence. The journey of discovery had begun.

CHAPTER SIX
SETTLING IN

BY SEPTEMBER 1937, when I arrived in London, England was beginning to exhibit signs of jitteriness. Stanley Baldwin, who had handled the abdication crisis of Edward VIII so well, had gone and Chamberlain was now Prime Minister with a large Tory majority. The politicians were forced to focus more and more on what Hitler was doing, and saying, in Germany. However, the predominant popular wish was to reach an accommodation with the German dictator. There were still vivid memories of the slaughter of the Great War and a resolve never to let it happen again. This mood was not lost on Hitler, who promptly annexed Austria in 1938, to the jubilation of the Austrian population. It is now acknowledged that the Chamberlain cabinet was deeply split on the German issue. One faction, under Lord Halifax, advocated accommodation at all costs, whilst others, like Eden, the foreign minister, and Churchill, at that time still out of Government, warned a largely indifferent nation of the Nazi threat.

Chamberlain, long maligned after the war as an appeaser, has in recent years had his reputation rehabilitated. Records of the time reveal that his Government started to consider the inevitable, another war with Germany. They also show that the Baldwin years had left the country woefully ill-prepared for such a conflict. Very late in the day, therefore, a number of crucial rearmament decisions were taken. The Spitfire project was started, with unprecedented orders for the RAF, and the vital radar stations were greatly enlarged until they covered the entire approaches to the country's coastlines. In the London parks storage shelters began to be erected and in every large field in south-east England concrete pillboxes sprang up like mushrooms against possible aircraft and glider landings. All this activity took

SETTLING IN

place in the greatest secrecy so as not to alarm the general public, who were still vehemently opposed to any military confrontation with Germany.

It was into this London that I was introduced in the autumn of 1937. My mother had returned to Berlin as she had not yet obtained her UK domicile visa. By that time, the government, fearing a flood of Jewish refugees, was deliberately restricting the issue of visas and many would-be immigrants were still waiting for the vital documents when war broke out. For the greater part they ended up in concentration camps, where few survived. This episode was a blot on England's liberal reputation and the stain on its character during the late 1930s regarding the official attitude to Jewish immigration is to this day not a welcome subject in official circles.

As a minor, I had received my entry visa, with the Joseph family acting as guarantors that I would not become a burden on the public purse. There was the immediate matter of where I was to live. The four Joseph brothers were all bachelors in an age range between twenty-eight (Teddy) and forty-one (Bertie). The two younger brothers still lived in the parental house in Hampstead, whilst the other two had their own flats. As Oscar had the largest and, moreover, still had their ancient nanny (Bunny) living with him, it was decided I should live there, where I would have some company during the day whilst Oscar worked in the family bank. This was strictly a short-term measure as the Josephs had already selected a boarding prep school for me, to which I went, half way through the winter term of 1937, by special arrangement with the headmaster.

My arrival at Falconbury School, at Cooden Beach near Bexhill, Sussex was something of a cause célèbre. The Josephs had failed to inform the school that, although fluent in German and French, I spoke hardly any English. This cut me off from my classmates, except as some kind of strange interloper. Fortunately, one master, the French teacher, took it upon himself to act as my interpreter. He translated everything into French and I replied likewise. German was not taught at the school. I owe a debt of gratitude to the patience of this young teacher, Mr Taylor, who was my lifeline for the first term. After the Christmas break, when I again repaired to Oscar's flat, my return to school coincided with an astonishing advance in my English language skills, absorbed in that enclosed atmosphere as if by osmosis. I was able to sit, and pass, the Common Entrance exam in the summer of the following year, 1938, without any language problem.

By that time Chamberlain had come and gone from Munich. Mussolini had conquered Abyssinia and in London gas masks were being issued. Despite the reprieve Chamberlain had wrung from Hitler at the expense of Czechoslovakia, the public mood had changed. At every level, preparations for an inevitable showdown with Germany were taking place and the atmosphere was one of false gaiety, as if people realised they were dancing on the edge of a precipice, determined to have one last fling before the curtains came down. Theatres, nightclubs, seaside resorts, all forms of public entertainment, were booming, yet the very evident preparations for war all around were a constant reminder of the approaching Armageddon.

In the summer of 1938 my mother was still in Berlin without a UK entry visa and, quite bizarrely, given the time and political situation, I was allowed to visit her during the summer holidays. Looking back, it was a huge gamble on my being able to leave Germany at the end of the holidays, but nothing untoward occurred. Through financial constraints, Mother had relocated into a much smaller flat and Berlin was now quite openly a very dangerous city for a Jewish boy. Most entertainments were out of bounds and so were public swimming pools and tennis courts. Miraculously, my mother still managed to run her small car, so we went out picnicking in the Grünewald or on the beach of the Wannsee.

On my return in September 1938, after taking the Common Entrance, I went to my public school, Felsted, again selected by the Josephs. My prep school had links with Felsted and quite a lot of boys went there from Falconbury. This practice was quite common; the whole stretch of coastal resorts between Eastbourne

SETTLING IN

and Hastings was peppered with prep schools and each had its own preferred affiliation with one or other of the boarding public schools.

Felsted was, and is, right in the middle of Essex, near Dunmow, and surrounded by huge sugarbeet fields. It was exposed to the east wind and, lying in flat terrain, it was very cold in winter. I only spent one year there as, early in 1940, we woke up one day to see several Bren gun carriers parked on our sacred first eleven cricket pitch. On those hallowed grounds only senior boys were allowed to walk. The Army had commandeered the school as part of its anti-invasion chain and the school was given only the length of the summer holidays of 1940 to find somewhere to relocate six hundred boys and all the staff. As our school was by no means the only one to be forcibly ejected in 1940, the competition for suitable sites and accommodation was intense. Some schools moved in with others, away from the danger zone, others found shelter in abbeys or abandoned country estates and a few closed altogether.

It was Felsted's good fortune to have at that time, as one of its alumni, a boy named Trafford. His family owned large tracts of Herefordshire and his mother put at the school's disposal three of her properties, all near Ross-on-Wye. The main building, which was to accommodate the four school 'houses' which had been in the main block at Felsted, was a Victorian mock castle, built to replicate a 14th-century baronial demesne. In its passages and turrets, its vast hall and innumerable attics, the masters organised classrooms and science labs, whilst the stores and outbuildings were converted into dormitories. The two former 'out' houses, one of which was mine, were more fortunate. One house was given Hill Court, a huge Palladian Regency villa, which possessed a tennis court and a pool and ample room for the boys' accommodation. The other house, in which I was and with fewer pupils, was allocated Pencraig Court, a delightful Edwardian manor house backing on to a road which runs along a ridge overlooking the Wye. It was altogether a great improvement on our Felsted accommodation. With ample grounds, a working grass tennis court and private access to the river below, we could hardly believe our good fortune.[67]

It had been decided from the outset that all tuition would take place in the main building, Goodrich Court; boys from the two outlying houses had to make their way there every day except weekends. In the case of my own house, Pencraig Court, this involved a leisurely cycle ride of about fifteen minutes but the other house, Hill Court, presented an altogether tougher challenge. Hill Court lay on the opposite side of the Wye to both Goodrich and Pencraig and when we settled in for the autumn term of 1940 two buses were hired, with sanctions for fuel from the Ministry of Transport, to ferry boys through Ross, via the main road bridge, and then up a very steep hill to Goodrich Court, an awkward journey of about twelve miles. All went relatively well until January 1941, when the buses were unable to get a grip on the icy road which led up the steep hill outside Ross and had to turn back. All appeals to the council for sand and grit went unanswered and it became clear that the school's problems were at the bottom of the many wartime demands which were suddenly heaped on the harassed council officers, who needed an influx like ours like a virulent disease. For the rest of that winter, the Hill Court boys went largely without any formal tuition and there was even talk of sending them back to London, which was then at the mercy of the Blitz. Fortunately, better sense prevailed and the next spring saw a cramming programme right through the Easter holidays, to bring the Hill Court contingent up to scratch.

Obviously, this experience preoccupied the masters and governors, who dreaded a repeat performance during the coming winter of 1941–2. Just at this point two masters, one with engineering qualifications, the other the head of the school's Scouts, came up with an extraordinary, even foolhardy, suggestion. Why not, they said, sling a pedestrian suspension bridge across the Wye at the nearest point between Hill Court and Goodrich?

67   In 1946 the school published *Felsted in Herefordshire* about the years spent in exile. *(Ed.)*

They had worked out precise drawings, weight ratios, wind resistance and cable strengths required for such a project. After much discussion and, in the absence of any alternative solution, they were given a very hesitant licence to go ahead. For the next four months a small army of masters, scouts and boys laboured to realise this truly remarkable construction.

By Christmas 1941 they had completed their task. It was made of a continuous length of two builders' planks, lashed together, side on side, to form a walkway wide enough for one person. He would hold on to either one of the two heavy steel suspension cables, carrying his school books with the other hand. When this proved too hazardous, large rucksacks were issued to every boy so that both hands were free to hold on for balance and support. The bridge was secured on one bank, which rose steeply from the river, by winding the cables around an ancient oak tree, which provided an anchor. The opposite side of the river was meadowland and required a heavy wooden gantry to be designed and erected so that the two sides were of equal height to take the suspension cables. It looked very much like a medieval trebuchet, without the bucket for the fire balls.

The test came on a windy winter's day with one of the two masters leading, followed by a volunteer from the boys (and there were many) and the second master bringing up the rear. In mid-transit a gust of wind swung the planks to and fro but by holding on tight the small party reached the other side, to the cheers of hundreds of boys and not a few locals as well.

Thereafter it became routine and, with regular checks and repairs, the bridge continued its daily lifeline throughout the rest of the war. Boys who used it became quite blasé and sprinted across without holding on and one intrepid individual even decided to cycle across. This exhibition of hubris angered whatever gods had protected us so far. The bicycle skidded and fell into the Wye, the boy fortunately held on to the cables and was unharmed except, that is, for the 'six of the best' he got from the Headmaster's cane for his exploits. In its next wartime edition, the Ordnance Survey map of Britain even marked the bridge on its maps of the Wye Valley, but in dotted lines, denoting a 'dangerous crossing.' Nevertheless, in all the years the school remained in Herefordshire, not a single boy fell from the bridge into the Wye thirty feet below.

THE TRANSITION TO Herefordshire opened up new vistas to many of the boys, who came largely from the Greater London area or the low lying flat lands of East Anglia. With the school scattered over three properties, magisterial supervision became nigh on impossible to maintain. The lack of suitable fields for sporting activities meant that only the top teams in each major sport could find space for competitive fixtures. The remainder either played tennis when they could or started to explore the countryside on their bicycles, drawing an ever wider arc for such outings, as far as Ludlow in the north down to Tintern Abbey and Chepstow in the south. We all had bicycles and they became our liberators. There were still sleepy hamlets that boasted the odd teashop where for a shilling or two the owner would serve up a full fry-up of bacon, eggs and sausage, washed down with lashings of tea, and that at a time when food rationing was beginning to bite severely.

It also spawned another activity which was strictly prohibited but could not be suppressed. The Trafford estate covered many acres of forest as well as mixed agricultural land and it was among the plantations of old Spanish chestnut trees that someone discovered a glorious way to exploit the wartime food shortage. Some boys came from farming stock and knew how to set snares. The land had had no rough shooting since the outbreak of war and most of the gamekeepers had been called up into the armed forces, leaving just two or three to look after huge tracts of land.

There soon developed several syndicates, each of three or four boys, who set traps and patrolled each one daily. Before long, contact with a local butcher in Ross was established, whereby he paid one shilling and sixpence for each adult rabbit. Wild meat was not rationed, whether venison or wild fowl, and even rabbits escaped the food rationing controls. Suddenly some boys

SETTLING IN

acquired considerable wealth by their poaching activities and even I, city born and bred, learned the skills of setting a good snare. Of course the masters knew what was going on but, as they were powerless to stop the practice, it went on largely undisturbed – until one day the senior gamekeeper's cat was caught in one of the snares. At that point all hell broke out and the entire school was threatened with eviction. One or two of the main practitioners were expelled and for the rest of the time that the school remained in Herefordshire no further rabbit snaring took place.

When I first arrived at Felsted, still in Essex in 1938, we juniors were housed in large dormitories and the few studies were reserved for the senior prefects. As a Victorian building, the place was already well past its prime, with outdoor WCs and very little heating. Much has been written about single sex boarding schools being incubators for homosexual tendencies. Leaving aside the more lurid accounts for which boys were expelled, these were few and far between. That is not to deny that among six hundred boys, crammed into confined sleeping areas, some mild form of mutual sexual experimentation occurred. It was largely regarded as a harmless form of the growing-up process.

There were, however, some very young boys among the latest intake, who had been cruelly separated from their parents at an early age. Some came from overseas civil service families, others were foreigners – and all were miserable. For lack of any other role model, they often developed a crush on the senior boys, and especially such figures as prefects or captains of sport. The attachments were often reciprocated by the older boys and clandestine love affairs developed that were spiritual rather than physical and were not exploited by the older boys in sexual dimensions. Rather, they gave the young entrants protection and some real friendships arose out of these early crushes. On the whole, it was a civilising influence in a generally bleak emotional environment.

Whilst this mild form of homosexual feeling was largely tolerated or ignored by the staff, it was a very different matter when it came to girls. Exposure to the opposite sex whilst the school was still in Essex was zero, except for the serving maids, young village girls who had better fish to fry than a band of snotty schoolboys. The transition to Ross brought about a subtle change, in so far as boys were allowed to go into the town on half holidays, for shopping or tea. Inevitably some boys suddenly awoke to the existence and attractions of members of the opposite sex by coming into contact with them in places like Woolworths, and one boy started a tentative affair with a shop assistant from that store. Nowadays this would be seen as a rite of passage, but when discovered, the Head-master, the Right Reverend Bickersteth,[68] an intolerant disciplinarian, made the poor lad walk in front of his car (for which he had a petrol allocation) all the way from Ross to Goodrich, about five miles, and then gave him a severe thrashing. It was only long after the war, when financial necessity forced single sex boys' boarding schools to admit girls, that a more civilising atmosphere began to change things for the better, and just in the nick of time for the continued viability of many schools.

---

68 Kenneth Julian Faithful Bickersteth (1885–1962). *(Ed.)*

CHAPTER SEVEN
THE BRITISH ARMY

FELSTED, LIKE MANY of its peers, took the Oxford and Cambridge School Certificates and Higher School Certificates a year early, so that by the end of the summer of 1942 I had no reason for remaining in the school. I was seventeen years old and had already decided to volunteer for the Army at seventeen and a half rather than wait for the call-up at eighteen.

This was a step I had decided to take for two reasons. The first was to avoid being drafted into the coal mines by lottery as a 'Bevin Boy,' so-called after Ernest Bevin, the Minister of Energy at the time. There was no appeal against this and the acute shortage of miners and the constant industrial unrest in the coal industry, even in wartime, meant that the government relied more and more on press-ganged labour for essential work. The second reason was to take advantage of a scheme whereby volunteers were allowed, within certain limits, to choose the branch of the services or regiment they wished to serve in. Waiting for the call-up usually meant ending up in the infantry, a prospect that appalled me.

When I opted for the Royal Armoured Corps my request was granted, and after a six-week initial training period, which everyone had to go through (about which more later), I was sent to Bovington Tank Training Centre in Dorset. Before starting on my tank course, however, I was posted to Glasgow's Mary Hill Barracks, a relic from World War One. It was a hutted encampment in one of the most deprived areas of Glasgow and the conditions of the camp and its huts were unbelievably squalid. We had wooden bunk beds, four men to each unit, and two straw-filled palliasses each. No blankets, no sheets, no lockers, all ablutions outside in a communal trough, in sub-zero temperatures (it was

December 1942).

There my so-far sheltered life received a rude shock. The other inmates were largely drawn from the dockyards of Liverpool and at first I could not understand a single word of their Scouse intonations. As their dialogue consisted mainly of swear words this did not matter, although my public school accent attracted much derision. One night, after lights out, I heard a rustling under my bunk and, throwing back the palliasse, uncovered a large rat. I had been cleaning my kit and fortunately had my bayonet sheath near to hand with which I gave the rat an almighty whack, thereby dispatching it to rat heaven. By this one act of self-preservation I won the respect of all the tough Scousers, who thereafter admitted me to their clan and taught me many lessons of survival which came in very useful later in the war.

All this time, I was still classified as an enemy alien, with a German passport alongside my new Army paybook and identity tags. Our Sergeant Major, a bemedalled veteran of the first war, had been chosen to break us in and gave no quarter for the slightest deviation from his high standard of what a 'proper' soldier should be. One day, after drill, he called me over and I could see he had my papers in his hand. Dreading the worst, I gingerly approached him expecting a tirade of abuse for some failure or other. Instead he looked at me rather quizzically and said, 'Laddie, it says here you are German, so what are you doing fighting against your own people?' I tried to explain my Jewish background, the Nazi persecution, my emigration and my gratitude for being able to enlist in the British Army. I don't think he understood a word but from that day he went out of his way to try to act as a father figure to me, no doubt thinking that I had more than one nut loose in the head and needed his protection. Looking back much later to those times, I could understand his puzzlement.

When the six-week induction training came to an end the Sergeant Major assembled us for a farewell address. He thought we were the biggest shower in all his army career but conceded that some of us might eventually make adequate soldiers. He warned us that during our postings we would meet many scheming

'Fräuleins' (girls of all foreign nationality were lumped together as Fräuleins). He told us that every one of these schemers had the pox and if we were not very careful we would end up with knobs as big and as red as billiard balls. After this piece of sex education he was quite overcome and might even have had a tear forming on his cheek. He came of a breed of men that was becoming extinct even then, with an innate decency and pride of country, of which the mould has long been broken.

Only two other events from that time filter down the years in my memory like silver threads in the well of an abandoned mineshaft. On New Year's Day the Scots celebrate Hogmanay. We were given the evening off and, armed with bottles of whisky, small groups of two or three soldiers would knock on the doors of the small Victorian terraced houses in the Mary Hill Road. The ritual was ancient and never varied. When the door opened one of us would thrust the bottle forward and invite the householder to have a 'wee dram'. At that we were ushered into the parlour where several bottles were already standing on a nearby table. We in turn were offered the liquid hospitality of the house, and I do not recall that our bottle was ever in use owing to the generosity of the people who plied us with drink until we passed out. I vaguely remember reclining, like Endymion, into deep slumber, under a table, but in place of a gourd tree I fell under the shadow of an enormous haggis before being dragged back to barracks.

The second occasion that still remains in my recollection of that bleak winter was a special concert given for the forces in the Grand Theatre, Glasgow by the legendary soprano Dame Eva Turner.[69] She was then in her fifties and well past her prime as one of Britain's greatest interwar interpreters of Wagner, although she still sang at Covent Garden for a year or two after the war. She gave us arias from *Turandot* and *Der Rosenkavalier* and the packed house, made up entirely of service personnel, brought down the rafters.

After some leave in London where the nightly bombing made for an uncomfortable time, I was posted to Bovington in

69 Dame Eva Turner (1892–1990). *(Ed.)*

Dorset. The barrack blocks there had only just been completed before the outbreak of war, under the Army's refurbishment programme initiated by Leslie Hore-Belisha (he of the beacons), at that time Minister of War.[70]

Coming from the mouldering huts of Mary Hill, we could hardly believe that this luxurious accommodation was to be our home for the next nine months. Although still in dormitories, we enjoyed showers and baths, recreation rooms, parquet flooring, central heating and very little square bashing, which featured so largely in our last camp. Instead we went to classes in engineering, radio telephony, truck assemblies, engine management and much else. The field tests for one's radio operator's badge involved map-reading and buzzing along the empty countryside in small Hillman vans, each equipped with the same two-way radios we would find in our tanks. It was stimulating work and only after completing these ancillary courses were we introduced to the tanks, in our case American Shermans. Learning to drive a forty-ton vehicle was exhausting but exhilarating and the gunnery practice that took place in Lulworth Cove was another new experience. We had to learn to be competent in each of the tasks carried out by the five-man crew so as to be interchangeable in times of need, a measure I was to be grateful for a few months later when the test of how well we had absorbed our lessons came in real combat situations.

On our twenty-four hour leave we would go to nearby Bournemouth, where we were welcomed in the many hotels that organised dances. During the war Bournemouth was full of girls, many from the services, others working as nurses, besides its own large indigenous population. Many of the hotels waived their charges for service people and it was not uncommon to take in three dance venues in the same afternoon or evening. The only problem was transport. The railways were expensive and with few civilian drivers on the roads, thumbing a lift was often a frustrating experience. In the end, four of us got together and

70 Leslie Hore-Belisha, a Liberal, was appointed Minister of Transport in 1934. He brought in the driving test and amber-coloured globe beacons at zebra crossings. *(Ed.)*

raised enough money between us to buy a car for shared use.

This was a 1932 Wolseley Hornet sports car similar to the MGs of the time. It managed to squeeze in four people (just) but we decided it would not long survive such heavy loads. We therefore split up so that two of us had the car one weekend and the other two the next. This arrangement worked perfectly well until the tyres, already bald when we bought the car, went down to the canvas and developed holes into which the inner tube then protruded and promptly burst. Tyres were as rare as hen's teeth in the middle of the war and being such an old car they were not even being made in that size any more.

We had to try every trick in the book to keep the car running. One was to cut up sections of disused tyres into patches which were called gaiters and then glued into the inside fabric of our tyres, covering the holes. This worked for a time but made for a very bumpy ride. Petrol was, of course, not available to the public, including troops' private vehicles, so we befriended a staff sergeant in the stores who, for a hefty consideration, provided a five-gallon jerry can of petrol. This was a most clandestine operation involving going out on Wool Heath in the middle of the night, to an allocated spot where the jerry can had been left well hidden by the supplier, to give him an honourable name he hardly merited. Still, with all the chicanery and black market spawned by the war in every sphere of life, this was a small deceit. One way or another it kept us motoring until our passing out parade nine months later, when each of us went our different ways and the car was sold to the next troop coming up after us. The only miracle was that none of us were injured or even killed driving such a decrepit vehicle.

We took the tanks out on public roads, bizarrely with an 'L' plate affixed to the rear, and on one occasion when I was driving with the instructor sitting alongside we came to the picturesque village of Corfe Castle. The road through it twisted around the ancient houses and, as a tank was steered by pulling on two levers, it was difficult to turn it gently. I misjudged one corner and hit an old timber frame of a corner house jutting out into the road.

The beam fell down and with it a good slice of the overhanging balcony. My instructor took one look and said laconically, 'Drive on, the Army will pay for the damage.' I thought I would be court martialled at the very least but, in the event, nothing more was said about it, at least to me.

At the end of the course I was a fully-fledged RT (radio telephone) operator and as such dispatched, after a week's home leave, to Harwich where a ferry took me to Ostende. After a few days there I was glad finally to be sent to my regiment, the Sherwood Rangers. This was September 1944, just after the Arnhem disaster.[71] The Sherwood Rangers had fought their way up to Holland all the way from El Alamein via Tunisia and then became one of three tank regiments to cross on D-Day. They were by then fitted out with DD Shermans, which were essentially floating tanks that depended on canvas screens to stay above water.

Two things went wrong. The Navy's tank landing ships launched the tanks much too far from the shore, a disgraceful and rare episode of loss of nerve by the senior service. Once in the water the seas were very choppy and soon lapped over the upper edge of the canvas screens. The tanks never had a chance and the regiment lost sixty per cent of its armour, through sinking, in one day. None of the crews escaped.

The second wave was more fortunate but by the end of July the fierce fighting around Caen had virtually wiped out the Rangers as an effective force. They were finally withdrawn and reinforced more or less from scratch with new officers and men. I was one of those reinforcements and joined the regiment near Nijmegen in Holland, where it was stuck fast. The failure to capture the vital bridge at Arnhem had left Montgomery's British and Canadian First Army group dangerously exposed about two hundred kilometres ahead of the main armies coming up through Normandy. Monty's dream of an end to the war by Christmas was in tatters.

---

71 Thousands of British and Polish troops were killed, wounded or taken prisoner in Operation Market Garden, a plan to seize bridges in the Dutch town of Arnhem. Winston Churchill lionised the courage of the fallen Allied soldiers with the epitaph 'Not in vain.'

THE BRITISH ARMY

Holland in that winter was literally starving. We were encamped outside the town and when the Germans blew up the dykes holding back the waters of the Zuider Zee the whole area was flooded. It was a thoroughly uncomfortable experience and lasted from September until February 1945. At Christmas news filtered through of a big German breakthrough in the Ardennes, with Antwerp its objective. They came perilously close to trapping the whole of Monty's Army way forward to the North. An almighty scramble to pull back ensued, no one knew what was happening, and it was mainly down to the brilliant tactical withdrawal by General Brian Horrocks, the corps commander, that we were eventually out of the trap. The Americans fought heroically at Bastogne and, outnumbered ten to one, held up the crack SS tank regiments long enough for the Allied air forces to intervene, finally, on Boxing Day, after clearance of the dense fog which had prevented all flying in the previous week. Unopposed in the skies, they decimated the German advancing tanks so that by New Year's Day 1945 the crisis was over. We were, by that time, in new locations near the German–Dutch border around Maastricht and in early February the Battle of the Reichswald Forest, on the approaches to the Rhine, began.

The fighting was the fiercest the regiment had faced. The Germans knew that they had to hold the Allied forces before they could cross the Rhine, and fought fanatically. We sustained serious losses and on 3 March, after two lucky escapes, when my tank was hit without the crew being injured, I was wounded by mortar fire whilst getting out for observation on the ground. I remember waking up in what turned out to be a Canadian Army ambulance. When I glanced across to the other stretcher I saw to my horror a wounded and unconscious SS officer, still armed with his Luger pistol. I banged on the partition which separated us from the driver's compartment and yelled that I was sharing the ambulance with a Nazi who would think nothing of using his pistol on me. The driver came to look and said that I need have no fear, the German would not make it to the field hospital, never mind shooting me, so I should stop worrying. This turned out to be true but it was a shock I could have done without.

The Canadian field hospital was in Holland, under canvas, and I was bandaged up and some of the larger metal splinters were removed. The next day I was taken again in a Canadian ambulance to a military landing strip near the town of 's-Hertogenbosch.[72] A Dakota DC3 air ambulance stood on the grass strip and, together with several other stretcher cases, I was loaded into the specially adapted aircraft. Without further ado we took off and an hour later landed at Brussels. From there I was taken to a brand new hospital which had been requisitioned by the military. The next day I was operated on and most of the shrapnel was removed.

On returning to the ward I was visited by the Lieutenant Colonel of the Royal Army Medical Corps, who had performed the operation. He held a wallet in his hand with a hole torn through the leather. He told me I was extremely lucky as the wallet, with its wad of occupation money from a successful poker game, had broken the force of a large splinter directly over the area of my heart where I had stowed it in the top pocket of the 'Zoot' suit which all tank crews wore and which were the envy of non-armoured regiments.

After about two weeks I was discharged to a convalescent home. This turned out to be one of the many hotels along the Belgian North Sea coast, a favourite holiday resort in pre-war days for its fine beaches. We were kitted out in bright blue suits with Army buttons. The colour was cornflower blue, the cloth made of thick serge and not very comfortable, especially in warm weather. These garments were a relic from the First World War and there was no escaping having to wear them. The entire coastline between Knockke at one end and Ostende at the other was dotted with recuperating members of the forces, as nearly every hotel had been taken over by the services and turned into a convalescent home. Those who could get about were free to do so as there was a total absence of discipline.

I was fortunate in that my wounds healed without complications and after a week or so I was able to take the tram,

72 Known to the Germans as Herzogenbusch. *(Ed.)*

which ran the whole length of the Belgian North Sea shoreline, to sandy beaches near Ostende. There was a large contingent of ATS (Auxiliary Territorial Service – the women's branch of the British Army) stationed nearby and they provided the very pleasant social environment we enjoyed.

After two more weeks I was pronounced fit and ready to rejoin my regiment. The war was in its final stages and after my home leave it was May and the war in Europe was over. Together with another recuperee we were given travel passes to a transit camp near Brussels. When we arrived there we found the few radio telephone operators in a state of turmoil. The end of the war had brought about a huge movement of troops and no one was sure exactly where the various regiments were on the day of the armistice.

A colleague who was in the 13/18th Hussars and I waited for two days for movement orders but none came. The harassed Captain in charge of the camp had only one objective, namely to disperse the sudden influx as quickly as possible. He asked if we could drive a Jeep and of course we said we could – after a Sherman a Jeep would be a doddle, or so we thought. He gave us a pass for the large transport pool to draw a Jeep and wished us good luck. He gave us a rough indication where our respective units might be found but with the daily deployment of all forces underway he could not guarantee that his information was still valid. We had heard, from troops returning to go on leave, that our regiments were in the most forward position of the Army, having halted somewhere on the west side of the River Elbe, facing the Russians who had advanced to the other side and were itching to cross over. Only the four-power agreement at Potsdam imposed a no-movement order on all armies until the final demarcation lines between the four zones could be ratified.

We knew nothing of all this as we filled our Jeep to the brim with petrol and started out on what turned out to be a fascinating ten-day journey across devastated Germany. We did not hurry and took every advantage of the free accommodation, food and company the traumatised German civilians thrust on us, as if we were the vanguard of a liberation army. All along our route, which took us roughly from the Ruhr district, south-east in the general direction of Hanover, over three hundred miles away, white flags or sheets fluttered from every window and not a single swastika was in sight. The overriding concern of these people, expressed to us again and again, was their fear of being occupied by the Russians, whose barbaric treatment of the east German population had been broadcast by the thousands of fleeing refugees trying to reach the Allies in the West.

We tended to avoid large towns in case the Military Police took too close an interest in our odyssey, and stayed in villages or small isolated inns. The locals were short of every commodity and a packet of cigarettes or a tin of army sausages would buy any favour, especially from the young female contingent. Often they had not seen a young man for years, as all able-bodied males had been conscripted and only the old and infirm remained. We usually headed first to the local Burgermeister's house, where we ordered him to collect all firearms held by farmers and others in his area of jurisdiction. We set a twenty-four hour deadline during which the locals vied with each other to offer us accommodation, and more. Promptly the next day we went back to inspect the haul. We were in for a surprise as large numbers of shotguns, rifles, pistols and even some grenades were stacked floor to ceiling.

There was no way we could take any of this ordnance with us in our Jeep, so we selected one good shotgun each, for recreational use, and made the Burgermeister sign an affidavit on pain of death to the effect that he would keep all the lethal hardware under lock and key until a proper occupying detachment from the Army was dispatched to his village, to whom he would hand over the arms. So compliant were the locals that I believe that no breaches took place, something I later had confirmed by troops stationed in the various villages we had passed through.

However, we were no nearer our destination. No one we met on the way knew where our units were and, whilst they offered us shelter, we did not want to be absorbed into a strange outfit for fear we might never be able to leave it. The journey continued. Living off the land and using our Belgian depot pass, we had no difficulty in getting petrol from the odd army unit we passed on our way. After ten days of vagabonding my colleague received news of the exact location of the 13/18th. This was in an area about forty miles east and we decided to go there to drop him off, leaving me with the Jeep but still no news of my regiment's position.

Luckily, the 13/18th, who had fought at our side since D-Day, knew where the Sherwood Rangers were halted. It was on the west bank of the Elbe near a town by the name of Aken. I had finally found my lodestar and set off without delay. The ten previous days had been great fun, albeit tinged with shock at the sight of some of the devastation. Now I just wanted to be back where I belonged. When I found one of the squadrons the next day, I reported to the Squadron Leader, who was most surprised to see me. He greeted me with the words, 'I thought you were dead.' Evidently this was the message he got when I was wounded, another instance of the communication breakdown at the end of the war. He welcomed me back but told me that the regiment was going to be disbanded, one of the first of the Yeomanry units to be culled, partly because of its long fighting history, from Egypt to Germany between 1941 and 1945, and partly as a result of a general demobilisation. He then told me that he was recommending me for OCTU, the Officers Training Unit and that I would be going back to England very soon.

Sure enough, a week later my movement order came through. I was to have a week's leave and then report to the Royal Armoured Corps OCTU, which was now based at Bovington, where I had trained a year earlier. Before reporting there, however, a telegram came to my home where I was on leave, to the effect that the Sherwood Rangers were to mount one last parade as a complete regiment, about six hundred in all. This was to honour a request by the city of Nottingham, whose Mayor and Council wanted to bestow their esteem, as a Nottinghamshire Yeomanry Regiment, by holding a thanksgiving service in one of Nottingham's major churches, St Mary's.

The whole regiment paraded through the streets of the city, which were lined with many waving and applauding spectators.

There followed the service and then some of us were invited by the Mayor into the large Council Chamber, where he bestowed, on the part of the Council, the freedom of the city on the regiment as a token of gratitude for its achievements and the pride in which it was held by the citizens of Nottingham. Each of us received a silver badge with the city's arms on one side and the regimental crest, a hunting horn, on the other. In practical terms, as collective freemen, we were told in the Mayoral address, we could drive sheep through the streets of the town although he begged us not to exercise this privilege too often as it would cause chaos to the traffic. After this ceremony the Sherwood Rangers were formally disbanded, most men went to Transit Camp for reposting to other units, whilst I reported to the OCTU adjutant at Bovington to start my officer training course.

This was normally a nine-month course but because of the shortage of junior officers it had been cut back to six months. We were distinguished in our dress code from lesser ranks by a round white disc worn behind the cap badge in our black berets. In all respects we were treated like officers and called 'Sir' by all lower ranks, including NCOs. Even the fierce Drill Sergeant Major who put us through our paces on the parade ground would call us 'Sir,' but only as a prelude to a round of abuse such as, for instance, 'You are a dreadful shower, Sir!' Half way through the course I developed shingles and was excused many of the more onerous exercises for nearly two months. Eventually most of us passed and officially received the King's Commission. This was marked by a great ceremony called the 'passing out parade'. Most cadets had already chosen a regiment they wished to join, either for hereditary reasons or because of some other connection. I was not too bothered and went into the 'pool.' Shortly after leaving Bovington I received my posting to the 12th Royal Lancers who were at that time in Egypt. I had a week to prepare, during which I equipped myself with tropical kit.

A couple of days before I was due to go to Southampton to embark for Port Said a telegram came through directing me to report to the War Office at once. When I finally got to the right section a Major in the Intelligence Corps told me that my regimental posting had been put on hold as I was needed most urgently as a native German speaker, to assist the Commandant of the Allied Control Commission in charge of the large city of Hanover. I was both annoyed and flattered but as I had no say in the matter I duly made my way to Hanover. I reported to the Commission's offices and was conducted to the Colonel, an amiable former university don. He was clearly at the end of his wits due to the total lawlessness in the town for which he was responsible. The German police had all been disbanded and were still going through a denazification process and the few British Military Police were overwhelmed.

The problem was not so much with the indigenous population of Hanover, who were largely law-abiding, albeit short of almost every necessity of life as a result of the almost total destruction of the city's infrastructure following the many thousands of bomber air raids by the RAF. Rather, the Commission's main difficulties came from the wave of DPs (displaced persons) who had fled westwards to escape the advancing Soviet armies. These included not only east Germans, but also Russian deserters, Polish farm labourers and Gypsies. As there was no accommodation for them and the Army did not recognise them as its responsibility, they roamed through the city, begging and stealing, the girls offering themselves for a chocolate bar, and some elements terrorising the population in the countryside. UNRRA (United Nations Relief and Rehabilitation Agency) was only just beginning to bring in emergency food supplies but such was the chaos that most of it was stolen by gangs who resold it, at huge profit, on the thriving black market. In practice this became so all-embracing that it became the only source of food and heating fuel, at a price which most ordinary citizens were unable to afford. Then there were the gangs, the Russian syndicates who would regularly murder members of their Polish counterparts, the Gypsies who denuded the farms of every living creature, and the small group of Allied soldiers who were drawn into this débâcle for the huge profits they could make by selling their Army rations, cigarettes and even ammunition. When caught they were court-martialled but the majority got away.

Into this inferno I was plunged, a total novice of twenty, with my language skills the only assets. The Colonel was so relieved to see me that he made me his ADC for Civilian Affairs. Every morning the Military Police brought in their trawl from the previous night and I was the conduit both for the prosecution and for the defence. By 8am, about thirty prostitutes would be in the corridors, smoking, crying or just doped to the eyeballs. Each one was herded into the office and the same routine began. We knew it was a futile attempt to impose some sort of order on the city and they knew it as well, so the whole procedure was a waste of time. As for the gangs, when the few careless ones to be apprehended were brought in the Colonel would despatch them to a newly erected holding camp outside the city where they came under the custody of the Military Police.

Side by side with responsibility for the civil administration of the city, the Intelligence Corps had circulated a list of wanted Nazi war criminals who had vanished in the confusion of the last days of the war. Our office had about twenty-five names, ranging from concentration camp commanders to SS money-launderers. As the Army did not provide the necessary manpower to hunt down these people there was not a lot we could do, except scrutinise any suspicious character who was caught on one of the trawls. One day a burly man was brought in on a charge of racketeering and the Colonel, who had a keen eye, told the guard to keep him in another room for processing later in the day. He then led me over to a large chart of mugshots or press photos culled from various intelligence sources, showing the faces of wanted men and a vague description of their physiques.

He pointed to one of these faces and asked me what I thought about the man held next door. I had to admit that I also found a strong resemblance, although the picture showed him in a high-ranking SS uniform, not the shabby clothes he now wore. We brought him back in and I began to translate the interrogation. He said he was a refugee farmer who had fled from the Russians. He admitted his involvement in the black market, for which he had been arrested. This did not satisfy the Colonel, who had obviously been well trained by some Secret Service organisation in spotting flaws in replies to interrogation. He brought out the chart and showed it to the prisoner, pointing to the particular photo showing the resemblance.

The man first went white as the blood drained from his face, then he turned puce and stuttered his vehement denials. I had to tell him that the Colonel was not satisfied with his replies and that he would be sent, under guard, to the British Army HQ at Herford for further questioning. At that the prisoner went berserk, yelling that we were all Jewish scum, possibly a tenable proposition in my case but certainly not the Colonel's, and that he was indeed the man on the chart and proud of his rank as an SS officer. He denied any knowledge of concentration camps, claiming to have been in a fighting unit of the SS on the eastern front.

Some weeks later we had a message from Intelligence HQ at Herford congratulating us on apprehending one of the most wanted war criminals on the Allied list, a notorious camp commander in Poland by the name of Schuler.[73] The Colonel was so pleased that he said, 'This calls for a small celebration.' He gave a cocktail party to which he invited officers from all the regiments in the area as well as members of the UNRRA team now stationed in the town. At this party I met Josie, a Bristol girl attached to UNRRA, holding a nominal rank of seniority much higher than mine. This did not however hinder our burgeoning relationship which endured for the rest of the time I was to spend in Hanover.

All good things having to come to an end, with the gradual improvement of the security situation and better supplies of essential food and life support necessities for the population, I was finally allowed to leave and join the 12th Lancers. Before I left, the Russian POW Major whom we had made Commandant,

---

[73] I have not been able to trace this man with any certainty. He may have been Robert Schuler, an SS leader, who hanged himself in February 1946 in his cell at the British Army of the Rhine HQ at Aachen while awaiting trial on war crimes. (*Ed.*)

on our behalf, of a large DP camp holding mainly Russian and Polish army POWs and their assorted dependants, threw a farewell party for all of us in the Control Commission. His followers had raided the countryside for days and, although we had heard of these activities and their intended purpose, we did not intervene. Moreover, we had heard something not yet known to the inmates of the camp, to the effect that they were all about to be dispatched back to the Soviet Union on a specially sealed train, under an agreement between the four occupying powers. This mean almost certain death or the Gulag for most of them and great care was taken that no leaks broke out about this operation.

The party, when it came, was something entirely outside my sheltered, civilised, Western experience. First we were seated around a vast table, each of us with a Russian or Polish neighbour on either side. Then the toasts began, all drunk in vodka. First to the great Soviet fatherland and Stalin, then to the King of Britain and the President of America. Curiously, De Gaulle and the French were left out; perhaps they had never heard of them. Then the female members of the camp came laden with huge trays of food, all the proceeds of the foraging of the previous days. Then there followed the music, on balalaikas, harmonicas and violins, and both the men and women took turns in ever wilder dancing, to the point of exhaustion. After many more toasts most of us westerners were comatose and if not yet under the table certainly in no condition to drive back to our base.

The Russian Major had prepared for this moment. He announced that as his honoured guests he could not possibly allow us to risk injury or worse by driving back and that he had prepared accommodation for all of us in the old dilapidated castle that lay inside the zone of their encampment. We were each ushered to a dank cell-like room, without electricity but provided with an acetylene lamp. Our hosts then bade us a very good night and departed. No sooner than the door had closed on our guide, I noticed someone else in the room. It turned out to be one of the Polish girls from the party who had been allocated to each of us as 'hostesses' for the night. Modesty forbids any further elaboration on events which followed, except that at breakfast the next morning a very badly overhung set of British officers could barely look each other in the eye.

Our party had included the Army Chaplain to the Commission, a Church of England padre of reticent demeanour. He eventually appeared but refused any food or drink and looked thoroughly miserable. To cheer him up one of our less inhibited officers told him of the night's adventures with the Polish girls provided by our hosts. At that he threw up his hands and wailed 'Only one girl? They set me up with two!' The poor man was certain that he would be drummed out of the Army and of the Church, although we were all convinced that he preserved his chastity against all odds and really deserved a medal for bravery in the line of duty. We concluded that the Russian sense of humour was very different to that we were accustomed to in our buttoned-up Western ways.

IN THE EARLY part of 1946 I was finally ready to join my new regiment. There were two or three cavalry units stationed in Egypt and Palestine and going out on the SS *Otranto*, an old but comfortable Orient Line ship, I found myself in the company of a few of my contemporaries at Bovington, which made for a stimulating journey. After ten days out of Southampton we landed at Port Said, then in temperatures of the high forties. We spent two nights in a transit camp and were then dispatched on a single-track train that ran parallel to the Suez Canal from Port Said to Suez. We got off at Port Tewfik, a pleasant oasis resort, built and still largely occupied by the French. This lay about five miles from the town of Suez at the southern entry to the canal.

Suez was indescribably foul and very hot, so we avoided it as much as possible. The regiment was encamped under canvas in various sized tents and marquees, for want of alternative accommodation. The regular officers, as distinct from our National Service commissions, still had a few horses and played a sort of desert polo, but the regiment's purpose was reconnaissance. It was equipped with Humber armoured cars, already obsolete before the war, and a few small two-man scout cars. There was not much to do in Egypt and we all anxiously awaited our next posting.

In my case this came about three months after arrival and the destination was Palestine, where the three squadrons were each allocated their own area of operation. HQ squadron was based in Ramallah, in what is now the West Bank. We lived in well-built barracks, erected before the war and, after Egypt, enjoyed the climate and proximity to the sea. At that time, the later troubles which ultimately led to the Jewish–Arab conflict of 1948 had not yet manifested themselves. Towns such as Jaffa were still wholly Arab populated whilst cities like Tel Aviv were Jewish. The most northerly city was Haifa, predominantly Jewish, with a fine harbour and a large Shell refinery. On the outskirts of the city the road wound its tortuous way up Mount Carmel from whose peak one had a magnificent view of the flat expanse of citrus groves and palm trees, with the Mediterranean in the other direction. One of our squadrons was stationed in Haifa and much envied by the others for this town's cosmopolitan attractions.

Life was generally relaxed. There was some riding, more sand polo, snipe shooting for a delicious breakfast treat and bridge with the Colonel, who was an avid follower of the game. A few subalterns who had foolishly admitted to playing bridge were frequently press-ganged to play against the CO and the second-in-command, a crusty old Major who had been in the first war as a young ensign and had taken part in one of the last cavalry charges of the British Army. The stakes were high; six old pence a hundred and far more than was within the financial resources of a second lieutenant on £4 17s. 6d. a week, out of which he had to pay his mess bills. Only by good fortune and the Colonel's habit of overbidding his hand did we juniors manage to balance the books in our favour.

Early in 1947 the first atrocities took place. The most notorious was the kidnapping by terrorists of three officers of the 11th Hussars, one of whom was executed by hanging. The perpetrators were thought to be members of the Irgun gang, an ultra-Zionist organisation whose objective was to try to drive the

British out of Palestine so that they could attack the Arabs without interference. This event left a traumatic mark on the mood of the Army and we were put on a high alert footing. Not long after these events the terrorists developed new tactics. A nightly sleeper train ran from Haifa to Cairo via the Kantara swing bridge over the Suez Canal. One night the locomotive was blown up by a bomb placed on the track in the countryside outside Haifa. Two more similar attacks followed within weeks, with the engine driver and his fireman killed in each attack. Not surprisingly, the railway employees went on strike until their safety could be guaranteed.

This task fell to the British Army and was solved in a typically British piece of ingenuity, albeit with many dangers attached. The solution which was adopted was to take the wheels off two old Humber armoured cars and in their place fit steel railway engine bogies. The converted cars would then precede the train with a fifteen-minute interval and detonate any mines before the train was due to pass. In practice, it was hoped that the armour underneath the chassis would absorb the shock of an explosion without killing the crew. Each evening this strange convoy set out from Haifa, much to the amusement of the Arab children lining the track, who did not understand the serious purpose of this odd parade. Either the terrorists felt they had made their point in the previous attacks or they decided not to risk a full showdown with the British Army. At any rate, no further incidents took place on the railway lines. Eventually the deteriorating political situation enforced a permanent suspension of this service, and so it has remained to the present day. When I reflect on these events I am saddened by the thought that no one will now experience the wonderful dawn when the nightly wagon-lits from Cairo to Haifa emerged out of the moonlit, freezing Sinai desert into the fragrant all-pervasive aroma of millions of orange blossoms, as it passed into the seemingly unending lines of citrus groves on both sides of the track.

Around the middle of 1947 the regiment was given orders to return to England within three months, the exact time depending on the worsening terrorist activity in parts of Palestine. One incident stands out in particular from the isolated incidents spread over the Protectorate in no discernible order. This was the blowing-up of the King David Hotel in Jerusalem by the Jewish underground Hagana movement. Its leader, Menachem Begin, became one of Israel's prime ministers many years later, but at the time he was Enemy No. 1 on the British list of wanted terrorists. The King David was Jerusalem's finest hotel and used by the British as their administration centre. The atrocity destroyed a large part of the building and resulted in heavy loss of life and injuries. It placed the Army on a war footing, whilst in London preparations were being drawn up for a total withdrawal from the territory and for the administration of the area to be handed over to the recently created United Nations. Our regiment's notice of evacuation marked the beginning of the implementation of this policy.

Before packing up the many items for shipment, except for the armoured vehicles, which would be handed over to our replacements, there was another matter to attend to. Like most Middle Eastern countries, Palestine had its fair share of stray dogs. With the troops stationed in what seemed a lengthy occupation, some of the NCOs adopted a number of these dogs and became very attached to them. This was not outside Army regulations but always with the proviso that no pets could accompany their temporary owners if and when they were moved to another posting. When the regiment received a firm date for moving to Port Said for embarkation back to England, the CO ordered the humane destruction of all personal pets. This very sad and unpleasant duty fell to the officers, who were equipped with revolvers, unlike the other men, who had rifles. When it came to my turn to put down my sergeant's crossbreed spaniel I simply could not bring myself to do it. Knowing that disobeying an order could be a court martial offence I pretended to shoot the mutt by firing over its head. This so frightened the wretched animal that it tore the lead out of my hand and bounded like lightning to the camp perimeter and out of sight. Fortunately, it did not return and thus my deceit was not uncovered. It remains in my memories far more traumatic than the earlier occasions when I had to fire in earnest on an anonymous enemy in battle.

In Egypt and Palestine we junior officers did not have a batman (soldier servant) as would have been the practice in Europe. Instead we had, each of us, the services of an Arab who was drawn from a vetted pool of local men who vied with each other for what was for them a most welcome source of income. My own servant, Ahmed, spoke practically no English. He drank my gin but performed his basic duties of shoe polishing, tea making and laundering adequately enough. When we were given notice of departure I had to explain to him that his services would no longer be required. This news produced a dramatic display of grief and much wailing. When he calmed down a little he suddenly brightened up as a brilliant idea came to him. He insisted, with little English and much gesturing, that he would accompany me back to England and continue serving his 'Effendi.' I tried to explain that England was a country far away, over the oceans, but he cut me short. He had heard England was at the end of the railway line to Egypt and that he would simply get on and off the train and continue as before, but this time in England. It was hard to shatter his illusion.

We returned to Port Said where we were to await the next ship for the UK, chartered by the Army. Other people have described Port Said better than I can claim to, except to avow that it was unremittingly foul in every respect and we counted the days with increasing desperation, waiting for news of transport. This finally came, ending several weeks in the worst place I have ever lived in to this day. We embarked on an Anchor Line passenger and cargo ship which came from India with freight but had its cabin and deck accommodation reserved for us. It was quite a small vessel, about ten thousand tons, and nothing like as comfortable as the old *Otranto* on which I had arrived a year earlier.

On the passage through Gibraltar and into the Bay of Biscay we ran into fierce gales and the unstabilised ship rolled perilously from side to side. Undaunted, our CO and his partner in bridge, the old Major, insisted that the nightly game should continue and he gave no quarter for such feeble excuses as seasickness. One evening, when I had been dragooned into playing, the ship gave such a severe lurch that the table and the cards were swept across the lounge. Everything fell to the ground but, totally unfazed, the CO ordered us to pick up the cards from the floor and replay the hand as if nothing untoward had happened. We arrived in Liverpool on a grey late summer's day and lined the rails to watch the unloading of the regiment's freight before we were allowed to disembark. Our quartermaster, a seasoned old-timer who had been commissioned from the ranks during World War Two, was in charge of packing up the many items that were part of the officers' mess.

High on his list was the ample supply of liquor which had been acquired, duty free, whilst the regiment was overseas. Despite strict orders from the Labour government of the day prohibiting the reimportation of wines and spirits into the UK under threat of punitive excise charges and possible civil or criminal prosecution, the QM had arranged to pack the many bottles of spirits into wooden crates on the outside of which the words 'Caution: Acid – Vehicle Batteries' were stencilled in large letters. All went well. We watched gleefully as crate upon crate was lowered on to the quayside by the dock cranes, and then one crate slipped its hawsers and landed clumsily on its side. We were horrified when moments later a trickle of colourless liquid started to seep out of the joints in the crate, forming puddles on the concrete quay. The handling dockers stood well clear of the crate and summoned someone who arrived with a large fire extinguisher and doused the whole area in foam. We never found out quite how many bottles of gin and vodka were sluiced into the Mersey but at least the Customs gave the rest of the crates a very wide berth and on the whole the enterprise counted as a successful coup.

We entrained for our next destination, a very long and tedious journey, through many war-damaged areas, to Bury St Edmunds. The older members of the regiment who had served in the war all the way from El Alamein and through Italy and who had not seen England for years were visibly shocked by the appalling scenes of deprivation and despoilation which suddenly confronted them.

Anyone with memories of 1947 and of the worst winter of the century, which had ended the previous year, will understand the trauma. Those of us who expected a joyful reception were rudely disabused. People were simply too tired and careworn to spare any emotion which went beyond the daily grind of a bankrupt nation. Rationing of all foodstuffs, heating fuel, clothes, petrol and even bread, the last freely available throughout the war years, was at its height and the black market was thriving.

One great scandal of the time, involving government ministers' dealings with a notorious racketeer by the name of Sidney Stanley, became such an embarrassment to the Attlee administration that a tribunal was set up in 1948 under Sir George Lynskey.[74] For any student of the period the transcript of the proceedings makes fascinating reading and encapsulates the mores of the times better than any researched account.

We settled down in old country houses and disused rectories and went slowly into peacetime mode. The release of service personnel had begun, slowly at first, and then developing into a torrent, as the longest-serving combatants were discharged in order of length of service and age. My own projected date for release was fixed for the end of 1947. I was offered, but declined, a short service commission in the new regular Army for another period of three years, with the substantive rank of Captain. I felt that civilian life had to be faced sooner or later and the protective shelter of Army life had to be relinquished before it became endemic.

1947 will be remembered for the major shift in the power struggle between the old western colonial powers who were trying to re-establish their authority in the far eastern territories that had been occupied by Japan and the new nationalist movements who wanted independence. In India the Attlee government decided to jump before being pushed, resulting in

---

74 The Lynskey tribunal inquired into allegations of corruption among British government ministers and civil servants. The allegations raised public alarm and disgust in the economic climate of austerity that prevailed in contemporary Britain. Though there were no prosecutions, the enquiry resulted in ministerial resignations. (*Ed.*)

the formation of Pakistan. In Malaya and the Dutch East Indies the European powers were still trying to resume their governing roles, leading to open revolt in many areas. In Malaya especially, the British were increasingly drawn into a cat-and-mouse conflict with the communist-led insurgents whose ability to outwit the British forces in the tropical jungle came close to success. The UK government decided to reinforce their presence in Malaya and Singapore and we were told that the regiment's next posting would be Malaya.

WHILST STILL IN Bury St Edmunds I was reaching the end of my Army service and only one more matter of personal interest stands out from that time. To go back a little, it needs to be put on record that throughout the war and whilst on active service with the British Army, with the ultimate rank in 1947 of 'acting' Captain, I was throughout classified as a 'friendly enemy alien.' Only the British could have invented such a face-saving title for ex-German refugees who had joined the forces. In 1938, whilst at school in Sussex, I had applied for naturalisation, a process which at that time took about five years. However, with the outbreak of war in 1939 all nationalisation applications were put on ice and their processing had only recommenced in 1946. One morning the post brought a large envelope bearing the crest of His Majesty's Home Office and addressed to Lt A. R. Oldham, 12th Royal Lancers c/o War Office, London SW.

This ministry had discovered the whereabouts of our regiment and forwarded the letter to me in Bury. It contained the confirmation of the success of my application for British citizenship and was accompanied by a certificate of naturalisation which would become effective upon my taking the oath of allegiance to HM the King before a Commissioner of Oaths who had to hear the formal affirmation and would then stamp the papers, rendering them valid.

I had to be accompanied by a witness in this ceremony and chose our adjutant, Robin Brockbank, who was then a Major and later went on to rise to the rank of Major-General.[75] He was one of the nicest men I had the privilege of knowing and he willingly agreed to be my witness. We looked up a solicitor's office in Bury and made an appointment with one of their Commissioners of Oaths. On the chosen day we turned up at their offices in our best dress uniforms, Robin wearing his Military Cross, won in the North African desert campaign in 1942, and I with my less glorious campaign ribbons for my war service in Europe.

After a few minutes in the waiting room we were ushered into the Commissioner's office. He had some papers in his hand and looked up as we approached his large desk. He motioned to two chairs facing him and then said that he thought there was some mistake and that he was expecting a German citizen by the name of Oldham or Oppenheim (he was unsure) for naturalisation affirmation and would we please explain what two officers of a renowned cavalry regiment of the British Army were doing by coming to his office.

I had briefed Robin on my background when I joined the regiment in Egypt and he knew what the meeting was all about. He kept an admirable straight face as I tried to explain to an ever more bemused Commissioner that there was no mistake, that I was the said German by the name of Oldham (ex-Oppenheim) and could we now please get on with the swearing in. He gulped and stuttered something to the effect that he could not understand how a British officer could have served all these years as a German alien, albeit 'friendly.' I still think he thought I was a German spy. The absurdity of the situation was clearly beyond his comprehension and with a sigh he read out the words of the oath of allegiance which I had to repeat. He then signed and

---

75 John Myles Brockbank (1921–2006), always known as Robin, was educated at Eton and Christ Church, Oxford, and was commissioned into the 12th Lancers in 1941. An obituary in *The Telegraph* includes the following anecdote. 'After being wounded in the action in which he won his MC, Brockbank found himself in the American base hospital in Alexandria. While convalescing he and a brother officer were wearing GI uniforms, all that were available, when General Eisenhower visited the hospital. "Ike" asked them whether they were not in the habit of saluting senior officers. Only when they had their hats on, he was told.' (*Ed*.)

stamped my papers and at that moment, on 2 September 1947, I became a British citizen. Robin congratulated me, as did the solicitor, and we went to the nearest pub, in all our finery, and I ordered a bottle of Champagne which Robin and I polished off, to the astonishment of the few regulars in the pub. On the way back to barracks in Robin's staff car I began to fear that my new-found status would be cut short by his adventurous driving, owing much no doubt to our celebrations. However, with many near misses and much honking from other affronted motorists we reached our base in good if somewhat unmilitary order.

I saw Robin once more in the 1960s when I was in America on business and he was Military Attaché to the British Embassy in Washington. He became a Deputy Lieutenant in his native and much loved Wiltshire and after his death in 2006 Wiltshire County Council named a hill and a valley near his home as Brockbank Point and Brockbank Valley as a tribute and in his memory. He was an inspirational officer with a deep feeling for the English countryside to which he contributed in countless ways throughout his life.

IN OCTOBER 1947 the regiment moved to the Army depot at Colchester, in preparation for the forthcoming expedition to Malaya. There were a number of training courses designed to help troops to fight effectively in the tropics. Most of these were theoretical rather than practical, for the good reason that jungle conditions could not be replicated in Essex. For my part I had at last been given my exact demobilisation date, in late November, and as I would not accompany the regiment to the Far East I was excused most of them.

With a few weeks to go to my release, and also the regiment's departure, I was kicking my heels without much purpose. By a stroke of luck the War Office sent a memo to all armoured units then stationed at Colchester in which they asked for an officer volunteer to take a number of tanks and armoured cars, British, American and captured German, to the large infantry base at Strensall in Yorkshire. The purpose of this expedition was to show the vehicles to the boys in the Army Cadet Corps who were encamped nearby. The appointed officer would have to have a knowledge of armoured warfare and an ability to demonstrate the various tanks and cars and to allow the cadets to operate them under supervision. This exercise was planned to last six weeks and would take me, if I succeeded in getting the job, almost exactly to my demobilisation date. I duly put in my request and was very pleased when it was granted.

The vehicles, about five tanks and three armoured cars, were being assembled at Aldershot for transportation by rail, on flatcars, to Yorkshire. A small halt on the line was chosen, near Thirsk, which was flat and suitable for the unloading. For my part I travelled separately by train and reported to the infantry Colonel of the depot at Strensall, Colonel Leveson-Gower.[76] He was none too pleased to see me, as Queen Elizabeth (later the Queen Mother) was scheduled to visit the depot and have lunch in the officers' mess. For several days, men had been deployed to tidy up the large compound and to paint everything that did not move a brilliant white in preparation for the royal visit. It was therefore hardly surprising that the colonel did not welcome a scruffy bunch of people, in our case myself, a sergeant and two lance corporals, who might detract from the pristine appearance of the camp. I had firm instructions to take the tanks to a field on the far side of the camp's perimeter where the Colonel hoped they would be out of sight.

On the morning of the Queen's visit a staff car met her at Thirsk station and drove her and her ADC the few miles to Strensall where a second guard of honour was waiting for her to arrive. At the main entrance to the camp she changed from her car into a Land Rover, in which she stood upright, holding onto a crossbar with one hand and waving to lines of cheering infantry soldiers with the other. The Colonel was at her side and they headed towards the officers' mess for the reception.

The road through the camp led over a slight rise before descending to the main buildings. When the convoy carrying the

76 Probably Harold Boscawen Leveson-Gower. (*Ed.*)

Queen reached the top of this elevation she suddenly asked the Colonel to stop the Land Rover. She had seen something peripheral which she wanted to examine. She had glimpsed the field and our vehicles and she wanted to take a closer look. We had been told to keep out of sight during the Royal visit and therefore stayed in our field, well away from the official ceremony. Whether our cover was blown by the Queen's sharp eye or whether she had heard of our presence I do not know. We were in our duty denim overalls doing some maintenance on the vehicles so as to be ready for the cadets who were expected the next day.

The Queen came up to us and we saluted, all the while getting black looks from the infantry escort whose schedule had been well and truly scuppered. The Queen went round all five tanks and was particularly interested in the German Mark IV Panzer which had been captured, intact, in North Africa and was still painted in the yellow desert colours. Unfortunately we were unable to drive it due to missing engine parts but we did invite the Queen to a drive in a half track, as her wish to go in a tank was made impossible by her attire. We drove around the field and on the road towards the main block and she thoroughly enjoyed the experience. Meanwhile the Colonel was following us in the official car and when we approached the perimeter of the camp the Queen told us to stop as she had to perform her scheduled visit. She transferred to the staff car after thanking us charmingly.

The upshot of this incident was a severe reprimand from the Colonel who felt that all his preparations had somehow been subverted by the unexpected interlude and he made great efforts to have us and our tanks removed from his camp. As our cadet training course was only for two weeks his wish was granted and we departed back to Aldershot.

CHAPTER EIGHT
TOWARDS AN
UNCERTAIN FUTURE

IT WAS NOW almost the date of my demobilisation and after a week back in Colchester I received the official letter to report to a nearby Army depot. Once there I had to hand over my revolver and received in return a two-piece suit, two white shirts, socks and underwear and a pair of black shoes. They also gave me a hat (a trilby I believe) and small necessities of life like shaving kit, soap and so on. I also received a large brown suitcase made of cheap fibreboard, into which all these items could be packed. Financially, the discharge bonus was £20 which was sent to me by way of a money order. The suits made for Army leavers came in two options. One was dark grey with thin stripes and the other a kind of peppercorn tweed in a mid-brown colour. I opted for the latter and took it to a tailor who altered it so that it came close to a reasonable fit.

And that was that. I had a travel pass to London, the last first-class ticket I would have for many years. Army rules allowed demobilised officers to wear their uniform for fourteen days after discharge and I took every advantage of this concession when I started to apply for interviews with prospective employers.

This process, and the sequence of what followed, is another chapter and not part of this account of my arrival in England, my school days and my four-year service in the Army. All in all, those ten years were for me the most challenging and rewarding of my life.

MARIA'S STORY

ESCAPE FROM BERLIN

THE FOLLOWING IS a deposition made by Alexander's mother Maria Oldham (née Pinner) in February 1977. Alexander transcribed it verbatim in German (to which Maria reverted at times, at the end of her life). The account shows how, despite the intervening forty years and a new life in England, the trauma of her flight and life as a refugee, never entirely left her.

I WAS BORN ON 5 SEPTEMBER 1891 in Frankfurt am Main, the second daughter of the Councillor Doktor Oskar Pinner, a renowned surgeon in Frankfurt. In 1913 I married Ernst Friedmann, the interior designer and member of the famous Hohenzollern arts and crafts practice Friedmann & Weber of Berlin. There were no children of the marriage and in 1921 I divorced Friedmann in order to marry the banker Robert Oppenheim, member of the Bank Hugo Oppenheim & Son, which was located in the Pariser Platz, next to the Brandenburg Gate in Berlin. Our son Alexander was born in January 1925. He lives in Wimbledon, is married to an English woman and has three children. He fought as a lieutenant on the British side during the world war, in the Royal Armoured Corps and in the 13th Royal Lancers, and he was wounded.

Unfortunately, my husband left me for his niece, Ehrentraut Petersen, the wife of his sweet nephew. My former husband changed his name to Opton when he emigrated and I changed my name to Oldham, the name taken by my son when he joined the British Army. My former husband emigrated to America in 1939[77]

[77] Robert Oppenheim actually left Germany in 1940.

and he died there, on 24 August 1956. His wife Ehrentraut died in America in November 1962.

My mother's sister was married to the [London] banker Leopold Joseph. They had four sons, of whom three founded, with their father, the bank Leopold Joseph & Sons. They provided guarantees for my mother, my sister (the famous artist and author Erna Pinner, who receives a German pension), my son Alexander and for me. My sister came to England in 1936. I brought my son to England and my Joseph cousins paid for his public school, Felsted in Essex. In order to hasten my emigration, I went back to Berlin and on arrival my passport was seized, and I discovered during a deeply unpleasant phone conversation with the customs investigation office that my bank account at Merck Finck (otherwise known as Dreyfus) had been seized so that, as the official said, I could not take the cash with me when I got an English visa. After these experiences I flew to Frankfurt and procured a valid passport and English visa for my mother, who immediately flew to London, abandoning all her possessions.

My mother died in 1944 and, following our enquiries, [it was apparent that] her collection of paintings, drawings and prints were drastically under-valued. We tried everything to show in our claim against the German Reich that the collection had been greatly under-valued but no other expert questioned Holzinger's report. So it was that my sister and I lost a great fortune, a huge sum by today's values.[78]

When my passport and all my money were seized, I found myself in a terrible situation. Dr Helmut Ruge[79] was my lawyer, but only I was able to apply for a passport.[80] It was 1938 and

---

78 See valuation and details of the portrait by Lovis Corinth, which was shown in the major edition of Corinth's work as owned by Councillor Pinner, and which is now in a private collection in Spain.

79 In her account Maria gave this man's name as Helmut Rugen, but he is more likely to be Helmut Ruge. After the war Ruge acted for plaintiffs suing for compensation for forced labour. *(Ed.)*

80 Maria means that she had to apply in person rather than commission her lawyer to apply.

everything appeared hopeless. For months, I went every day to the passport office – still no passport, just like in Manetti's opera *The Consul*. In order to emigrate I needed an 'export licence' but with every attempt came demands for more money. No money, no passport. But until the end of my life I shall never forget what I saw and experienced on 9 November 1938.[81] I was greatly helped by my maid, Friedl Graupner (who still lives in Berlin at 1000 Berlin 62, Gustav Nuellerstrasse 5). I write to her, and visited her in 1965. She went to tremendous efforts for me and I have only her to thank for the arrival in London of my furniture and pictures, etc, before the war.

After my divorce, I lived at Blumeshof in Berlin and then for nine months before my emigration in the Van der Heydstrasse. It was on 22 November 1938, although how I still don't know, that I received my passport. I went at once to the British consulate because I knew that getting a visa was a long process. The consul advised me to fly to England immediately. When I got back to the flat, my Friedl said that a Frau Sorge had telephoned. She rang again and said that she had lived in the same building in Blumeshof as me and had heard that I was leaving for England. She said she was a Party member and would do everything she could to prevent me going and she had written a denunciation of me because I had spoken out against her beloved Führer. That dark, damp night I went with my Friedl to see this Frau Sorge to try to persuade her not to carry out her threat but there were dreadful scenes and Friedl advised me to leave. I was confused and said to Friedl that all I could do was to throw myself into the Landwehr Canal near to Blumeshof, but my loyal Friedl said, 'Dear lady, you have your passport and visa, you must go now.'

I had the good fortune to have met an Englishman by the name

---

81 Kristallnacht ('Night of Broken Glass'), so called for the shattered glass from shop windows that carpeted German streets, signalled the start of a wave of pogroms against Germany's Jews. In the space of a few hours, thousands of synagogues and Jewish businesses and homes were damaged or destroyed. *(Ed.)*

of Bergel[82] (now dead), who was a diplomat in the mission for the non-intervention pact with Spain in London, and his flat was extra-territorial. I rang him and my lawyer and both came. I rang Lufthansa and found that the next flight to London was at 8am on 23 November 1938. Because I had sold my car on the black market I could buy a ticket, which I did, and I packed, I think, thirteen pieces of luggage and disappeared with them and four fur coats to the Englishman's flat, and also took my jewellery (although most of it was in Switzerland). Because I was going to be denounced, I did all this in a great rush. Around 7am I bade farewell to Friedl and the Englishman, and asked him, as soon as he saw my plane take off, to telephone my family in London to tell them I was coming – they did not know that I had been able to get a visa and had been sending telegram after telegram to urge me to come.

When I got to the check-in, I gave the official a thousand marks, and he let everything through. At the customs barrier, an SS guard asked how much money I had with me, and I replied, 'Only what is permitted, around fifteen marks, I think.' But as soon as I had boarded, over the airfield loudspeaker I heard a call for Frau Oppenheim to return to be body searched. For me, that was a certain route to the concentration camp. The denunciation must have come through. I was taken with all my things to a cell where a Nazi female guard told me to undress.

Out of fear, in the rush, I had forgotten to remove a brooch or a ring, so I awaited my fate. I told the woman that she could search me. However, she was staring at my open passport, and she said, 'Pinner... Pinner... was your maiden name Pinner?' I said yes. 'From southern Germany?' I said, yes, from Frankfurt. She said, 'Did you know Councillor Pinner?' I said, he was my father. She asked, 'How is that dear man?' I said, he had, praise the old, died in 1927, but how did she know my father? She said, 'I was a nurse in the infirmary where your father operated.' My father had been consultant surgeon during the First World War for the 5th Armoured Corps from Frankfurt to Cologne and this Nazi woman

---

82   Possibly David S. Bergel, a tobacco merchant. *(Ed.)*

had been a nurse there. She said that she was so sorry that I had to be searched, and asked: 'Madam, what can I do for you?' I asked her if she could get me and all my belongings on that plane and make what excuses she wanted to the SS. That is exactly what she did, and that is how I managed to fly to London instead of being sent to a concentration camp.

It is an unbelievable story, but all true. Of course, that and the hardships of building a new life with no money had a detrimental effect on my health, especially in my old age.

I arrived in England on 23 November 1938. My family gave me £5 per week. So began my life of putting a shilling in the slot in an ice-cold room – but happily not in the concentration camp. Although I had my furniture, I was not able to rent a flat. Dr Ruge asked for professional references but of course I had to say I had none. Finally, just before the war, I received my work permit and got a job working for a dealer in Old Masters in Bond Street. After working there for two years, I moved to the flat where I still live. At that time, I paid £120 a month in rent, including heating and hot water, but now I have to pay £1000.

In 1943, when the bombs fell on London, I followed my mother to Harrogate in Yorkshire and worked as a kind of commercial traveller for an interior decorating company which made all sorts of goods for Heal's, Harrods and so on. I was very successful and, after my mother died in 1944, I returned to London and worked for six years for that company, where I was badly paid but learned a great deal. I needed to sell many of my things but, with a loan of £250 (which I soon paid back), I set up my own business as a freelance interior decorator and between 1950 and 1973 earned enough not to have to sell anything further although, in 1972, I did sell my jewellery at Sotheby's, under the name of Mrs R. H. Oppenheim, and bought an annuity which, although it has been devalued by inflation, will be paid until I die. I live now off that annuity, my old age pension, share income, reparation money from Berlin and the very low income from my father's estate. It adds up to a relatively small amount.

I am eighty-five years old and should, because of everything that I lost to the Nazis (although it ended miraculously), not have any worries and be able to have at least a small pension from Germany. It is depressing to know that many people (I know of two) receive large pensions because of good connections or misrepresentations, and also those who are German citizens and not Jewish.

This, I swear, is the truth of my case.

Maria H. Oldham

Alexander in the British Army

Milton Keynes UK
Ingram Content Group UK Ltd.
UKHW040629181123
432822UK00004B/67